OUT OF WORK –

ANNE LOVELL is one of
problem page writers and bro
lor and voluntary worker, she
aunt' on *Bella* magazine since

Her first book, *When Your Child Comes Out*, was published by Sheldon Press in 1995.

Overcoming Common Problems Series

For a full list of titles please contact
Sheldon Press, Marylebone Road, London NW1 4DU

The Assertiveness Workbook
A plan for busy women
JOANNA GUTMANN

Beating the Comfort Trap
DR WINDY DRYDEN AND JACK GORDON

Birth Over Thirty Five
SHEILA KITZINGER

Body Language
How to read others' thoughts by their gestures
ALLAN PEASE

Body Language in Relationships
DAVID COHEN

Calm Down
How to cope with frustration and anger
DR PAUL HAUCK

Cancer – A Family Affair
NEVILLE SHONE

Comfort for Depression
JANET HORWOOD

Coping Successfully with Hayfever
DR ROBERT YOUNGSON

Coping Successfully with Migraine
SUE DYSON

Coping Successfully with Pain
NEVILLE SHONE

Coping Successfully with PMS
KAREN EVENNETT

Coping Successfully with Panic Attacks
SHIRLEY TRICKETT

Coping Successfully with Prostate Problems
ROSY REYNOLDS

Coping Successfully with Your Hyperactive Child
DR PAUL CARSON

Coping Successfully with Your Irritable Bowel
ROSEMARY NICOL

Coping Successfully with Your Second Child
FIONA MARSHALL

Coping with Anxiety and Depression
SHIRLEY TRICKETT

Coping with Blushing
DR ROBERT EDELMANN

Coping with Bronchitis and Emphysema
DR TOM SMITH

Coping with Candida
SHIRLEY TRICKETT

Coping with Chronic Fatigue
TRUDIE CHALDER

Coping with Cot Death
SARAH MURPHY

Coping with Crushes
ANITA NAIK

Coping with Cystitis
CAROLINE CLAYTON

Coping with Depression and Elation
DR PATRICK McKEON

Coping with Postnatal Depression
FIONA MARSHALL

Coping with Psoriasis
PROFESSOR RONALD MARKS

Coping with Schizophrenia
DR STEVEN JONES AND DR FRANK TALLIS

Coping with Strokes
DR TOM SMITH

Coping with Suicide
DR DONALD SCOTT

Coping with Thyroid Problems
DR JOAN GOMEZ

Coping with Thrush
CAROLINE CLAYTON

Curing Arthritis Exercise Book
MARGARET HILLS AND JANET HORWOOD

Curing Arthritis Diet Book
MARGARET HILLS

Curing Arthritis – The Drug-Free Way
MARGARET HILLS

Overcoming Common Problems Series

Curing Arthritis
More ways to a drug-free life
MARGARET HILLS

Curing Illness – The Drug-Free Way
MARGARET HILLS

Depression
DR PAUL HAUCK

Divorce and Separation
Every woman's guide to a new life
ANGELA WILLANS

Don't Blame Me!
How to stop blaming yourself and other people
TONY GOUGH

Everything Parents Should Know About Drugs
SARAH LAWSON

Family First Aid and Emergency Handbook
DR ANDREW STANWAY

Getting Along with People
DIANNE DOUBTFIRE

Getting the Best for Your Bad Back
DR ANTHONY CAMPBELL

Good Stress Guide, The
MARY HARTLEY

Heart Attacks – Prevent and Survive
DR TOM SMITH

Helping Children Cope with Bullying
SARAH LAWSON

Helping Children Cope with Divorce
ROSEMARY WELLS

Helping Children Cope with Grief
ROSEMARY WELLS

Hold Your Head Up High
DR PAUL HAUCK

How to Be Your Own Best Friend
DR PAUL HAUCK

How to Cope when the Going Gets Tough
DR WINDY DRYDEN AND JACK GORDON

How to Cope with Bulimia
DR JOAN GOMEZ

How to Cope with Difficult People
ALAN HOUEL WITH CHRISTIAN GODEFROY

How to Cope with Splitting Up
VERA PEIFFER

How to Cope with Stress
DR PETER TYRER

How to Cope with your Child's Allergies
DR PAUL CARSON

How to Do What You Want to Do
DR PAUL HAUCK

How to Improve Your Confidence
DR KENNETH HAMBLY

How to Interview and Be Interviewed
MICHELE BROWN AND GYLES BRANDRETH

How to Keep Your Cholesterol in Check
DR ROBERT POVEY

How to Love and Be Loved
DR PAUL HAUCK

How to Pass Your Driving Test
DONALD RIDLAND

How to Stand up for Yourself
DR PAUL HAUCK

How to Start a Conversation and Make Friends
DON GABOR

How to Stop Smoking
GEORGE TARGET

How to Stop Worrying
DR FRANK TALLIS

How to Survive Your Teenagers
SHEILA DAINOW

How to Untangle Your Emotional Knots
DR WINDY DRYDEN AND JACK GORDON

How to Write a Successful CV
JOANNA GUTMANN

Hysterectomy
SUZIE HAYMAN

Is HRT Right for You?
DR ANNE MACGREGOR

The Incredible Sulk
DR WINDY DRYDEN

The Irritable Bowel Diet Book
ROSEMARY NICOL

The Irritable Bowel Stress Book
ROSEMARY NICOL

Overcoming Common Problems Series

Jealousy
DR PAUL HAUCK

Learning to Live with Multiple Sclerosis
DR ROBERT POVEY, ROBIN DOWIE
AND GILLIAN PRETT

Living Through Personal Crisis
ANN KAISER STEARNS

Living with Asthma
DR ROBERT YOUNGSON

Living with Diabetes
DR JOAN GOMEZ

Living with Grief
DR TONY LAKE

Living with High Blood Pressure
DR TOM SMITH

Making the Most of Loving
GILL COX AND SHEILA DAINOW

Making the Most of Yourself
GILL COX AND SHEILA DAINOW

Menopause
RAEWYN MACKENZIE

Migraine Diet Book, The
SUE DYSON

Motor Neurone Disease – A Family Affair
DR DAVID OLIVER

The Nervous Person's Companion
DR KENNETH HAMBLY

Overcoming Guilt
DR WINDY DRYDEN

Overcoming Stress
DR VERNON COLEMAN

The Parkinson's Disease Handbook
DR RICHARD GODWIN-AUSTEN

Sleep Like a Dream – The Drug-Free Way
ROSEMARY NICOL

Subfertility Handbook, The
VIRGINIA IRONSIDE AND SARAH BIGGS

Talking About Anorexia
How to cope with life without starving
MAROUSHKA MONRO

Talking About Miscarriage
SARAH MURPHY

Ten Steps to Positive Living
DR WINDY DRYDEN

Think Your Way to Happiness
DR WINDY DRYDEN AND JACK GORDON

Understanding Obsessions and Compulsions
A self-help manual
DR FRANK TALLIS

Understanding Your Personality
Myers-Briggs and more
PATRICIA HEDGES

A Weight Off Your Mind
How to stop worrying about your body size
SUE DYSON

When your Child Comes Out
ANNE LOVELL

You and Your Varicose Veins
DR PATRICIA GILBERT

To Bob, with love

Contents

	Acknowledgements	x
	Introduction	1
1	Thank you and goodbye	5
2	The first effects – the first two weeks	12
3	The children	24
4	How the other half feels	32
5	Taking stock	44
6	What can I do to help?	56
7	Getting help and helping yourself	65
8	Adjustments	77
9	Positive thinking	88
10	Solutions and resolutions	95
	Appendix: The danger signs	105
	Further reading	111
	Useful addresses	112
	Index	115

Acknowledgements

There are many people to thank for their help and encouragement to write this book, but first I'd like to thank Sylvia Boyd, for writing to me at *Bella* and giving me the idea. I'm sorry that after I had replied, I was unable to contact her again.

Colin and Wendy Turner, whom my partner and I met at their Hampshire B&B, have been generous with their time and made many thoughtful contributions. We have followed their story since the day Colin was made redundant.

I also talked to Vanessa and Julian, to AG, a Senior Human Resource Manager, and AB, a radio Producer, about their personal experiences.

Vicky Maud faxed me a mile of information from her files!

I spent a morning with Sean, Eileen, Kathy and David, who are all counsellors with Relate in Northampton, and I'm extremely grateful for their time and willingness to help. Denise Knowles, spokesperson for Relate, set this up for me, contributed and has always been a great help.

Sally Davies and Frances Cook, of Sanders & Sidney, introduced me to the world of outplacement counselling.

Peter Trigg and Michele Cozzi at Drake Beam Morin PLC, international consultants in the management of human resources, were very encouraging and sent me their most up-to-date research and information.

I'm especially grateful to my school friend Clare Stronge and also Michael Witcher of Witcher-Stronge Selection in Surrey, who took me under their wings, gave me a good deal of their time and also helped check the material later. And then, of course, there is Bob, without whom I doubt if this book ever would have been started, and who chained me to the computer to get it finished!

Introduction

Dear Anne

My husband has just been made redundant, along with a thousand other men with British Coal. He has worked there for over 20 years.

I would be grateful for any advice on what problems are likely to arise and how I can help him to deal with them.

As I am not working myself, we will both be in the house together most of the time (help!) (ha! ha!). I was thinking whether I could do a college course, so we can both have a bit of our own space. My husband has gone from working seven days a week to nothing, but he has many interests, so I think that will keep him going for a while.

He is 40 and I am 37. We have three children.

I'd really like some help to know what he's going through.

Yours most gratefully.

Sylvia

PS: He's started reading *Bella* from cover to cover!

I received this letter in February 1994. It brought the reality of the news about massive job losses in mining, which I'd been reading about in the papers and seeing on TV, into sharp focus. Here was a real person – an ordinary wife, wondering how she and her family would cope with an extraordinary, new and strange situation – asking me for advice and help.

I replied about three weeks later, when her letter reached the top of the pile, and I remember finding myself floundering. I could encourage her to talk about what was going on with her husband and to try to share whatever decisions they felt they needed to make. I could suggest asking advice from the local Citizens Advice Bureau, their Bank Manager or Building Society about their changed financial situation. I could endorse her tentative ideas about taking up a course at a local college, either as a way of enhancing her own skills in case they decided she should become the chief wage earner or to give her an escape from the house if she needed it now her husband was around most of the day. I could agree that her husband's wide interests would help him cope with the new increase in leisuretime he now had. But, beyond that, what could I say that would help and how could I advise her about the problems she sensed might lie ahead?

Very often when replying to readers, I tend to give an opinion or suggest options and then give information about a self-help group or organization with specialized experience in the area the reader is enquiring about. As an agony aunt, I have referral directories and contact books going back over more than 11 years, so it's unusual for me to find myself unable to suggest a source of further information or help. There's also often a book I can tell the reader about, which will both reassure and inform them more than anyone could do in a letter.

When I was writing to Sylvia, though, I found that there was *no* self-help support group for families out of work, let alone a suitable book I could tell her about that would help her go through the problems her husband was facing as well as help them all, as a family, face the new problems of living with redundancy and unemployment.

There are any number of books to help individuals deal with the practicalities of living without work or finding a new job, writing CVs and dealing with psychometric testing. Some cover feelings and emotions, such as rejection and loss of confidence, but I couldn't find one I could recommend to Sylvia that might answer her questions or help them manage. So, I decided to write one.

My partner, whom I will call Michael Powell, has some experience of both redundancy and unemployment and is, anyway, of a much more practical nature than I. So, in a sense, we typify one of the basic differences between men and women and the way we all cope with difficult and stressful situations like unemployment. He wants to find ways of finding the answers and solving the problems, while I'm concerned with how I feel and think about the problem – and why. Michael's view of redundancy is included throughout the book.

Together, we have worked on this book, which is designed to be a handbook – a survival guide for anyone who, like Sylvia and her husband and family, are faced with a new and frightening situation that will inevitably change their lives for ever.

This book won't give all the answers to everyone because everyone is different and everyone's situation, personality, experience and way of life is different. The way we cope with any problem depends, I believe, on the sort of person we are and how well-equipped we have become to face life and all its ups and downs.

The way you cope with redundancy and unemployment in your family and in your relationship will depend on the sort of people you are and the strength of the relationship you had together before you hit this problem. And it is a massive problem! As Jenny Cozens, a Chartered Clinical Psychologist as well as an advice columnist, firmly states in her book, *To Have and To Hold* (Pan, 1995), 'If there is anything that psychologists have proved without any question at all, it is that being unemployed creates psychological symptoms, rather than the other way

INTRODUCTION

around.' So, there are certainly difficulties and dangers ahead for anyone who becomes redundant, as well as risks for their relationship.

As a senior human resource manager said, with feeling, 'Writing this book, you've taken on what is perhaps the biggest tragedy of the 1980s and 1990s, and it's one which people, especially politicians, don't want to have to talk about because it's supposed to be just a passing phase. It's not!'

During the earlier research period for this book, I found myself becoming more and more concerned that it wouldn't be able to offer much hope. But, as time went on, I was encouraged to persevere with it – in the same way that anyone living with unemployment is encouraged to persevere with coping and adjusting.

This book won't change your personality or give you coping skills you haven't already been blessed with or acquired, but we hope it will give you some ideas, some information and encouragement to help you survive this major change in your life and make something worthwhile and positive come of it.

1
Thank you and goodbye

John and Sally

The day that John was made redundant started badly. He and Sally, his wife, had argued the night before over the amount of money she was spending on clothes for the children and when he left for work, there was a stony silence between them. The drive to his office was short but stressful. He missed the last parking space and had to look for a meter. This would mean moving the car every four hours. He cursed.

But, less than two hours later, John was back at his car in a state of shock.

Redundancy – that happened to others, not to him! He had been with the company for 18 years. Yet, as he sat there and watched his tears fall on to the letter and the cheque he held in his hands, he knew it *had* happened to him.

The rest of the day was a blur and, when he finally went home at his usual time, he couldn't bring himself to tell Sally. Instead he had a bath, said he felt unwell and went to bed.

Next day, he left the house at 8 am as usual and spent the day drifting between the bank, the Jobcentre and employment agencies.

This was to be the pattern for nearly three months. He felt ashamed of losing his job and couldn't bring himself to tell Sally. Each day he hoped he'd find work and then promised himself he would tell her.

How long this would have gone on had fate not intervened is hard to imagine. Sally had noticed a change in John over the weeks. He had become tense, nervous and looked ill. As hard as she tried, she could not get out of him what was wrong.

One cold morning in December, John woke with the symptoms of flu and was too unwell even to get out of bed. Sally told him she was sending for the doctor, but not that she was telephoning his work to say he wasn't well enough to come in. She could not believe it when John's embarrassed ex-boss told her John had not worked there for three months.

When the doctor arrived, he had to deal first with Sally because she was in a terrible state. Her shock soon turned to anger, but John was too ill for her to say anything to him. For a week she looked after him, saying nothing. When she did, it was a huge relief to them both.

This is just one of the many tales we heard about how the shock of being made redundant hits people. There are *many* people, but particularly men, who come home and are quite unable to tell their partners they've lost their jobs.

There is often a feeling of shame. A terrible feeling that he is to blame for having lost his job. So, rather than admit to it – to his partner or, indeed, to himself – he would prefer to pretend that nothing has changed.

There are all sorts of confusing and conflicting emotions churning around here. Even though he's an adult and often a father, the loss of his job takes him back to the feelings of being a child who has been caught out doing something wrong and is punished for it. His partner seems to take on the role of parent and he's afraid to tell her what he's done, because he fears her anger, criticism or disappointment in him.

He feels ashamed, also, of being without a job. He may fear that his partner will love and respect him less because he is unemployed.

And, of course, there is the fear of poverty – or of not being able to give his family what he would like to give them, what they need and deserve or what they demand – and this can create an overwhelming anxiety.

John and Sally had been arguing about money and he was criticizing her. He may have felt an added reluctance to admit to his redundancy and thus open himself up to *her* criticism of *him* because of this. In their case, the relationship was basically strong and, once John's attack of flu was over, they were able to talk and plan together.

John now says, nine months later, that the redundancy 'made them review their lives' and, if anything, their relationship is stronger than ever. He has found a job as an office administrator and says he could never have succeeded in achieving this without the help and support of his wife.

Sally, too, had to deal with shock. For her, it was not only the shock of discovering that John had lost his job, but also the realization that he had been unable to tell her and had been hiding it and deceiving her for three months. There was anger in her reaction, too. But some of that anger may have been at herself, both for being blind to what was going on and for not allowing John to feel able to confide in her. For some couples, this would have been a trauma from which it would have been difficult to emerge. There might have been blame and recrimination on both sides. But, fortunately, John and Sally were able to work out a way of getting through the shock of unemployment together, which in itself helped John to find new work.

Colin and Wendy

When Colin walked in the door that Thursday afternoon, Wendy said, 'You don't look very happy.'

'Well, no. I don't feel very happy. I've just been made redundant. I've lost my job.'

Wendy was just about to leave the house to take the children to the dentist. She said she'd cancel the appointments, but Colin said, 'No – life has to go on.'

When she got back home with the children, she said Colin started talking in the kitchen about what had happened. Wendy doesn't remember what it was they were saying, but Colin suddenly turned and walked out of the room. She reacted with, 'Oh God – you always do this, don't you? We start talking about something serious and you walk off!'

Colin turned back and said, 'Don't you start getting at me! I nearly put the car through a brick wall this afternoon, I can tell you!'

Wendy heard warning bells. She felt she had to watch what she said because if she told him how she felt it would upset him more than ever.

I asked her if she thought Colin would *really* have considered killing himself on the drive back home. She said he'd had 150 miles to drive and the thought had certainly gone through his mind. 'What was he doing to do? How could he face going on? It would be easier just to finish it all.' She doesn't know what it was that brought him back to reality and to the front gate in one piece.

Colin took a week to tell Wendy what had happened when he'd been called into the Sales Manager's office that morning. And he only told her when they went together to talk to a neighbour who was a Personnel Manager. She was able to ask the questions Wendy hadn't felt able to ask.

Colin had gone into Head Office expecting to discuss a sale but the Manager had called him into his office and offered him a cup of coffee. Colin had just had one, so he refused.

'Well then, we'll get straight to the matter in hand,' said the Manager. 'Here's your letter. You've been made redundant.'

'What now?' exclaimed Colin, to which the Manager replied, 'Do you want to talk about it?'

'Well, you've obviously made up your mind. That's the end of that. You've written the letter. You've written out the cheque. It's a *fait accompli*.'

Wendy thinks, in retrospect, that Colin feels he didn't give the man a chance to explain, but then he hadn't led into it, he hadn't gone about it the right way. There was no time to take it all in, to cope with the shock.

So, then the Manager really laid into Colin and said, 'Well then, if you won't talk about it we want XYZ from you and ABC out of your car.'

So, Colin gave it all to him, slammed the car door, did a wheelspin and was off.

Thinking about this later, Wendy mused on what might have happened on that 150-mile drive back to their home. And if Colin *had* driven his car straight into a brick wall, how would the man who had just sacked him have felt?

'It's a life and death situation', Wendy thinks. You don't give a thought to how the other person is feeling at the time or what they're thinking, but later it can help to think about these things.

'I think they're unprepared [to give someone the sack] and probably as much ill at ease as the receivers are. But bearing in mind the devastating effect the redundancy is going to have on someone's life – and you *are* playing with lives here – I think they should take their responsibilities much more seriously. It's not just a question of passing the foul deed down the line. The MD doesn't want to do it, so he tells the next boss down, "You get so-and-so in and tell him we don't need him any more, he's redundant". I don't think that's acceptable. To say somebody needs training to do this might sound a bit over the top. But when you're dealing with people's lives, it's important.'

In fact, it isn't in the least 'over the top' to expect that a manager should be trained to make staff redundant, sack them, dehire them or whatever jargon phrase or word is used, and there are several choices.

Fifty ways to say it

According to recruitment consultants Drake Beam Morin, there are over 50 ways to tell staff you're getting rid of them. 'Don't come in on Monday' is fairly straightforward, but downsized, dehired or outsourced, let alone job-eliminated, canned, re-engineered or deselected, or, worst of all, career plateaued are just some of the expressions managers have used to cover their own embarrassment and uneasiness.

When it happens to you, you don't much care about how the boss is feeling, but as one TV executive, who was made redundant himself when he was in his early thirties, told me, you should be a better manager once you've been made redundant. Even so, when you find yourself, some years later, in the position where you have to make staff redundant, it's much easier to do it than to have it done to you.

THANK YOU AND GOODBYE

The biggest tragedy

But right now, when you've just lost your job or just heard that your partner has, that's of little interest.

There are many things that will have changed since that moment when you were made redundant and many that will never, ever be the same again.

You're not alone – millions of people have gone through the same experience as you and, even if bothering about anyone else's situation is the last thing you're interested in at the moment, it is worth taking a deep breath and thinking through some of the hard realities of life and work in Britain in the 1990s.

The realities

Many people will tell you, in order to try and help, that it's seldom the *person* who's made redundant, it's the position or job that is lost. Usually it's a structural exercise. Even if it doesn't help the way you feel, it's true!

The world of work has changed. To quote a Senior Human Resource Manager, who herself has been made redundant, 'It's the biggest tragedy of the 1980s and 90s.'

This woman, now employed in a large national organization, says that:

> redundancy is a national tragedy and it's one nobody, especially in Government, really wants to talk about. For politicians it's supposed to be a passing phase. But it isn't. And it's now far too easy for companies to make people redundant. Whereas when it all first started companies used to think about what they were doing, they don't any more. Executives at the top feel that people are just not important. It's happening more and more – a few thousand every week. People blame the Government, but it's the way businesses choose to run themselves.

Michael Witcher, of Witcher-Stronge Selection, puts it like this: 'There's been a great deal of delayering.' He describes the structure of companies in the past as being like a triangle: you started on the bottom layer and worked your way up towards the top until you became a general manager. But, all that has changed. All the huge corporate offices have gone, so that multilayered structure has been taken out.

To put it another way, as the TV producer said, 'if you've climbed up the mountain, there's less space at the summit. If you're "taken out", it's likely you'll have to go back down the mountain where the space available is a little wider and broader'.

THANK YOU AND GOODBYE

There's no such thing as a job for life

A great many of the people I've talked to while working on this book could only paint a bleak picture of the work and job situation in Britain right now. Everyone's agreed that now, there's no such thing as a 'job for life', and never will be again.

In the past, when children were at school, they were encouraged to work hard, get as many good grades in exams as possible, then go on to achieve qualifications or train for a trade or profession of some kind so that, at the end of their education, they could get 'a good job', and that was that. Also, apart from historic changes in the British economy and way of work, such as dock closures, the demise of ship building and, more recently, coalfield closures, most people expected to stay in their jobs for as long as they wanted to. Unless you were caught pilfering from the till or committed some major error or misdemeanour, you were safe. But not now.

When huge companies or works – such as a coal mine – close down, there are hundreds and thousands of people put out of work, all at once. Sometimes, whole mining villages become empty, ghostly places because, eventually, no one can afford to live where there is no work.

I remember driving along the road that goes through the mining towns in South Wales, between Glyn Neath and Abergavenny, through Merthyr Tydfil and Ebbw Vale, on the way back from a family summer holiday and realizing that these dark-looking, depressing and run-down places were once busy and filled with men, women and children going about normal daily life.

Because the idea for this book came from a miner's wife, I talked to Relate counsellors, especially in the Northampton area, who have worked with couples for whom unemployment has become part of their relationship problems. In many cases, counsellors felt that because mining communities suffered redundancies on a major scale, there was an in-built loyalty and a great deal of social support and mutual understanding for the whole group of people made redundant and their families. There's a sense of equality, a team spirit, a feeling of people working together to combat a common 'enemy' – unemployment.

A male counsellor pointed out that, in a mining community, miners will tend to be sons and grandsons of miners, and their wives may also follow this pattern through the generations, so there will be family and community skills to draw on for coping with bad times. There'll be a history of knowing how to 'tighten the belt', like the stories and pictures of miners picking bits of coal off the slag heaps or from the beach.

Miners, for instance, often have well-developed social structures. There are things to do as a group, clubs of all sorts – from pigeon racing, dogs or fishing to meeting at the allotments. These all give a structure to life that is unaffected by the loss of work and costs very little.

There'll be group support and, perhaps, group efforts to help each other. A miner or factory worker, therefore, lives and works in a group. A car mechanic, however, is likely to be self-employed, work alone and be isolated from other workers.

Having a structure, a framework, for our lives is important for most of us. If we grow up in a family group, we're provided with a basic surrounding framework. We go to school and we're in another structure where we know our place, we know what we have to do, where to go and there's even a special language that includes us and makes us feel secure. Then, you may join other groups as you grow up – the Scouts or Guides, cadet corps, the local brass band – and these make us feel 'one of the gang'. It's a kind of tribal instinct that seems to be necessary for most human beings. When you get a job, you're often a part of a group there, too, and close friendships can develop at work that are quite separate from friendships outside, at home or in the family.

When you lose that job and leave the group, you're on your own. As Michael Witcher graphically commented, 'When you walk out of the office door, it's as if the waters close over your head and you were never there.'

Things are changing

Even 10 or 15 years ago, many people felt embarrassed to admit that they were out of work, but now, we should all expect to have to change jobs several times during a 30 to 40-year working life. So, if you, or your partner, are now among the ranks of 'the unemployed' – a statistic, one of a huge group that has been called 'Major's millions' – you're not alone! Take heart and start rethinking and planning for change. For, if nothing else is certain, it's certain there are changes ahead.

2
The first effects – the first two weeks

My partner, Michael's view of redundancy

Why me?

Even if you've picked up on all the signs, you'll still be wondering why you're the one who's been singled out for the sack. Of course, there could be others, sometimes thousands, but redundancy is a very personal thing – you can't share it with other people. You may all be the victims of the same event, but your reaction will depend on who and what you are as a person.

It's best not to ask for an explanation. If a reason has been given, it's probably a neutral party line. It may even have been prepared on the basis of legal advice, in which event nobody is likely to add anything of consequence that might be used later at a tribunal or in civil action. Accept that there is nothing you can do to change the situation.

Are you getting a fair deal?

The answer can only be 'No'! If life were fair, somebody else would have been made redundant instead of you. That aside, the real issue is whether or not the financial compensation you receive is appropriate, given your contract of employment, age and length of service.

At the start of the current recession, many employers were embarrassed at having to make redundancies and that generated a kind of 'fair play' in compensation arrangements – employers wanted to be viewed as compassionate bosses. Now that the slump has lasted so long, such a concern is not so evident, except that there is an enormous growth in the work of outplacement counsellors, who are used, as a Human Resource Manager, AG, said, 'so companies can think they're kind and caring'. AG went on to say:

> There's even a lot of counselling now for people who have *not* been made redundant. Apparently the feeling is now that if you've made a lot of people redundant, the people left behind are filled with such guilt and stress – guilt because they're glad it wasn't them and stress because it might be them next time and what's happening to their fellows – that they need counselling.

There also seems to be a rule these days that if you're not up to giving people the sack, you may not be up to doing the job.

Severance packages

It's fair to say that today very few severance packages – outside the public sector or the former nationalized industries – offer any more than the minimum statutory or contractual entitlements.

Statutory redundancy payments are calculated on the number of years you have worked for your employer and your age on leaving.

If you are aged between 18 and 21, you'll get half a week's pay for each year of service.

Up to the age of 40 you're entitled to one week's pay for each year of service and after the age of 40, the entitlement increases to $1\frac{1}{2}$ (one and a half) weeks' pay for each year of service.

Contractual entitlements

These will depend on the precise wording of your employment contract and the provisions of any related documents, such as the rules of the company pension scheme.

Pensions These are the one area in which the greatest liberties are taken. Many schemes provide for contributions to be frozen in the event of departure before normal retirement age and provide no facility for either inflation or continuing contributions. For those who started working before the advent of portable private pensions, the disadvantages are immense and need to be borne in mind in any contractual negotiations.

If you are a member of a final pay scheme (a scheme in which your pension will be calculated on the basis of the number of years' service in relation to your final salary), its real value is likely to be substantially higher than its current transfer value, assuming normal investment criteria.

Fringe benefits The area of fringe benefits is another that needs to be carefully considered in the calculation of compensation payments. The rule is that compensation is payable according to the loss of benefit. This means, for example, that if you enjoy the benefit of a company car or private medical insurance, the benefit you lose is the cost to you, as an individual, of replacing that facility and not, as is often the case, the cost that the employer would have incurred if you had remained in their employ.

If the sums are substantial, litigation may be worth while. For those of us who are not trade union members, however, the costs are generally too prohibitive for such a course of action to be contemplated.

The Government Actuary has taken account of the real value of loss of pension entitlement in the formula used in connection with awards, following successful claims for wrongful dismissal. It is worth remembering that many 'pay in lieu of notice' arrangements are outside the scope of employment contracts and this can be a useful negotiating point when considering the pension issue.

It may be worth asking a consulting actuary to assess your precise situation and advise you on the wisest course of action. The Association of Consulting Actuaries (Tel: 0171–248 3163) (see Useful addresses) will give you a list of members who are prepared to advise privately.

Anne's view

The first few days are probably the hardest to cope with. It's all so new, so strange and so frightening for both partners – the one who's lost their job and the one who feels all the same fears, shares the same worries but feels utterly powerless to do anything. Women who are based at home with children are likely to feel this the worst. Those who have a job to go to can 'get away' for a few hours at least – even if this makes them feel guilty at leaving their partner behind.

'It's like walking on egg shells,' said one woman, talking of how the relationship feels in the first days after a redundancy.

Helen had two young children and had reduced her job in the National Health Service to part time when her husband, Chris, was made redundant the first time. She remembers:

> There's so much anger and a feeling of betrayal by the company he'd worked his guts out for. But it's easier for that anger to be directed at you, than at them.

Wendy told me:

> I really had to watch what I said and make sure I didn't ask too many questions. I had to wait for him to talk, and it wasn't until about a week later that I got the full story. I don't know why. Whether it was because he didn't *want* to talk about it or didn't think I was interested or it didn't concern me or he didn't want to worry me. But it wasn't until we went to talk to someone we knew, who's a Personnel Manager for a firm of accountants. She really pressed him with lots of questions. I found out a lot more then that I hadn't known. I don't know if that's commonplace with all chaps . . .

For many men, it is much easier to talk to someone who's detached, who doesn't know him intimately, about something that has affected him so violently. And someone who's trained to ask constructive questions will be able to help him bring out all the feelings he may have felt afraid to admit to in front of his partner.

Colin had had a week to think on his own and let some of the worst of his reactions die down. He told me of a man he'd talked to who said that his response to the loss of his job had been to 'go to ground for a month'. He said he hadn't answered the phone, he'd just hidden away and 'gone to pieces'. This man, who'd become a regular visitor as a B&B customer, was single and living alone.

Colin didn't know what had brought him out of this state – he hadn't asked – but he was very supportive when Colin told him he'd lost his job. He told Colin that the worst thing he could do was 'hide in a corner'.

Colin, being a natural salesman, had instinctively let people know he was out of work and looking for something new, which was the right thing to do.

One of the people he had told was an acquaintance who ran a garden centre and stone yard. He'd been a customer of Colin's. The previous summer, Colin had helped him out by taking a couple of days' holiday to mind this man's business so he could get away with his family. This man told Colin that he'd been thinking about expanding his business to offer a garden landscaping service. He'd want someone to run the office side of things so he could go out to customers. He asked Colin to come over to talk about the idea and the outcome was the offer of a job – at a couple of thousand pounds less than Colin had been earning, plus a second-hand car. He agreed to take it.

Colin came back home, bearing this news, and found some friends and their children playing round the swimming pool he'd built in their garden. 'Everyone made him feel wonderful by congratulating him and he felt good that he'd been well-received and applauded', said Wendy, later.

So, within a week of being out of work, Colin had found a new job! Wendy said:

We don't feel it's a permanent thing. It's something to keep going on with for the time being. I can handle that better and I think Colin will. But the good feeling is that, when the real need was there, he got something else almost straight away. If it comes to an end, say, in four or five months' time, we'll be prepared for it and have had a chance to think about a few more ideas. Colin hasn't had to touch his redundancy money because he hasn't needed to. With what he got in wages, and being paid a couple of weeks later, he's covered the mortgage payments out of the bank. So in a way, it's been a sort of cooling off period, at a time when he needed his confidence boosting, which is great for him. Because that's what it's about, isn't it – losing your job. You lose your self-confidence.

Loss of confidence

That's it in a nutshell. Even an apparently supremely confident person suffers a terrible loss of self-confidence and, worse still, self-respect when they're thrown out of work through no fault of their own. Men, especially, often feel that the ground they stood on has been torn away from under their feet. Anyone whose confidence is thin or merely a surface veneer will feel completely stripped and worthless at such a time.

For many people, an outward appearance of confidence has been hard-won in adulthood after a childhood when no one made any effort to praise or encourage. Consequently, they grew up believing they weren't very clever or good enough – beliefs that stay deeply buried, however thick the coating of surface confidence may have been painted. For these people, any real success or achievement in life is tempered by an underlying belief that, one day, someone will find them out.

If you, or your partner, is someone for whom this is true, then the blow to the confidence will come even harder than it does to most people.

Coping capabilities

The way we cope with any shock or trauma in life depends, to a large extent, on the person we are or have made ourselves into. Whatever has happened in our life beforehand plays a great part in our reactions to things. So, if you've been through a major trauma, the bereavement of someone close to you or other loss in the past and survived, when you go through another, like losing your job and livelihood, you're likely to be able to cope rather better than someone for whom such a major life event is a completely new thing.

It also helps if, along the way, you've gained some self-awareness – you know a bit about yourself and how and why you behave and react in the ways you do.

Coping as a couple

This applies to your relationship, too.

If you are a well-established team and always have been, then there's a much better chance that you'll cope with the shock of redundancy and the threat of unemployment as well as all the changes and adjustments that will have to be made if the situation goes on for any length of time.

Teamwork – it's the only way to cope. *There's absolutely no doubt that the only way to get through this situation is to work as a team – both as a couple and as a family.*

THE FIRST EFFECTS – THE FIRST TWO WEEKS

You're both shaken and struggling with fears and worries of your own, but, somehow, you have to merge those together and construct a plan of action to get you all through the first days and then weeks, possibly months.

In 1994, the average length of time out of work for redundant executives surveyed annually by human resources management consultants Drake Beam Morin, was 5.6 months. This represented a 7 per cent drop in the figure for the previous year.

If, like Colin, you find another job to go to within a week, you may heave a sigh of relief and believe your troubles are over, but they may not be. It's worth remaining in a state of readiness for any eventuality and doing the planning anyway.

John, who also found a new job within a week of being made redundant, made a few adjustments, like buying a cheap, second-hand car that they could afford to run to replace the expensive, rather flashy car he'd been given as part of his pay-off. Otherwise, though, he and Vicky behaved – and still behave – as if losing his job was merely a hiccup!

The fact that they're both young, both working and so far without children may have a lot to do with this, but John says that he decided not to take out redundancy insurance when they bought their present flat, 'because I now have far more confidence in myself and my ability to get a new job if it happens again'.

Their form of teamwork is that of one personality complementing the other. John describes himself as 'rather a laid back person' and Vicky felt she had to motivate him into getting a new job quickly. 'The way she reacted was the best thing for me,' John said afterwards, 'and it all worked out for the best.'

The first fortnight

Many people have told me that if there is no new job to go to after a week or so, the first two weeks feel like a holiday and it's tempting to treat them this way. Obviously, most of us are used to taking this amount of time off work for our annual holiday and, indeed, when there has been a reasonable pay-off, severance pay or redundancy payment, there's a good argument for making the most of such a breathing space to relax and get away from the stress of the new situation.

If you can do that – or your redundancy happens in the summer and your holiday is already booked and paid for – then why not? Holidays – or at least a break from routine and preferably away from home – are essential for most of us to recover from the everyday stresses of life, even in normal circumstances. In this *abnormal* circumstance, and after suffering a shock, it may be just what you need. That is, as long as you can relax enough to make the holiday worth while and don't spend all your time worrying, with sleepless nights or drinking to drown your sorrows!

A holiday is something that can go on the agenda for the planning and discussion that must take place between you in these first, crucial weeks (see Chapter 5).

Sex

This is by no means a book about sex, but it is a very important part of any couple's relationship. As agony aunts often say, sex isn't the most important part of a good relationship, but if it goes wrong or there's a problem with it, it's bound to affect everything else. Sex is the glue that holds it together.

Sex can often be seen as a reflection of what else is going on in the relationship and, indeed, it can be used as a weapon by one partner against the other to achieve something that doesn't appear to be achievable any other way. Sex can also be used to say something to a partner without words. It's meant to say, 'I love you, I want you, I think you're exciting and attractive, you turn me on, we're good together', and all the other things two people who make love want to express to each other. But, it can also say other things and be used in other ways. One wife told me:

> I felt I had to give a lot more physical love and I think bedtime relationships, if anything, had to be increased because you need to have this sort of rapport between yourselves. You need to say you still need him, you love him and that side of his 'manhood' is OK.

'Don't forget the sex side', said Helen at the end of a long interview about the two redundancies she and her husband Chris had been through. She said that Chris wanted sex all the time – every night and whenever the children were out of the way – especially the first time he lost his job. At first she enjoyed it, but, after a while, when she began to feel that his increased sexual urge had little to do with his emotional feelings for her, she admitted it became a bit of a chore.

A male counsellor in Northampton pointed out that:

> A good bonk reminds you that you're a man and that relates and equates very quickly to work – the two things that remind you you're a man, work and sex – that's what you're there for. As long as you're doing both those things, you're a man. If you stop doing one of those things, you start to wonder just what you are. You start having doubts about yourself. You're asking, I'm not going out to work, but am I still working? Can I still get it up?

THE FIRST EFFECTS – THE FIRST TWO WEEKS

A female counsellor said she'd noticed with some clients that the husband becomes very demanding sexually:

> After years and years of not thinking about sex much, suddenly he wants to do it three times a *day* instead of three times a *month*. The wife wonders what on earth is happening. Is this the man I've lived with for the last 20 years? She feels completely baffled by the sudden increase in desire for sex. She also feels used. It feels to her as if he's got nothing else to do, so he'll bonk the wife.

So, an increased desire for sex is quite common and quite normal, especially for men who have suddenly lost their place in the world of work. Understanding this and being able to respond, for a partner, may make their life more exciting and more enjoyable. One woman said, a month after her partner lost his job:

> We go to bed a lot earlier and there's an increased interest in nookie. But I've always been an 'available' woman. I've always been of the opinion that if they can't get it at home they'll start looking for it elsewhere. I'd sooner be a willing partner than find out I'm in competition with someone else. It's not becoming a chore – no, not really.
>
> When you've been with a man for 12 years you know them very well, you know what turns them on, but it doesn't take as long. It used to be hours when we first got together – now an hour would be remarkable!

It says something, I think, about this couple's relationship that she is seeing her compliance with his sexual needs as a way of maintaining the relationship, a means of holding on to him. A sex therapist might contend that she is giving in to him in a somewhat condescending way and not sufficiently considering her own needs. On the other hand, however, she would probably say that she prefers the prospect of being with him in the long term to being without him, and certainly of having to fight to keep him!

We are all meeting our own, often unacknowledged needs in any relationship – sexual or not. An Alcoholism Counsellor at Relate in Northampton remembered a couple who had found a way through the wife's drink problems and she'd 'got sober' a couple of years before her husband was suddenly made redundant. She was getting on with life and working again, but from home. When her husband was left without work, she described him as the 'moper at home type'. So, they were stuck at home together, getting on each other's nerves. They came to

Relate for counselling because the husband said his wife had gone off sex since she stopped drinking, but, in fact, the problem was that he was now at home all the time, wanting sex. They worked through that, with help, but later other problems overtook them. They're still together, but struggling.

Another counsellor had noticed that some men, who are not as desperately destroyed by the redundancy, but actually find they quite like being at home or taking the home-based role, also find an increased interest in sex. Perhaps, he says, because they've got more time to themselves, without the pressures of going out to work, they feel more relaxed and they want more sex. If their partner has returned to full-time work to make up the money, when she comes home at the end of the day and he wants sex, she just isn't in the mood. She's too tired, she's too busy and there's too much to do. So, arguments and conflict start up as a result.

Both partners need to be even more sensitive to each other's sexual needs and feelings than ever. And, of course, you have to talk about feelings long before they *become* a problem.

Real problems

One of the other male counsellors at Relate in Northampton pointed out that:

> People get very tied up with these feelings of confidence and ability. They try very hard to believe that 'I've been made redundant not because I wasn't able or any good at my job but more because of money or that I was superfluous.' But that's not the *internal* thinking they're carrying round with them. They feel very much that they've failed – that they *weren't* good enough at their job, that they *weren't* able to do the job they were asked to do. And those feelings filter down into their sex life. So, sometimes they'll find there's a loss of erection or sex becomes all very hurried or they become premature ejaculaters – they come too quickly.

Loss of libido, loss of interest in sex, occasional loss of erection, difficulty in getting and keeping an erection or periods of impotence, are quite common experiences for men who have been made redundant.

This, of course, is a problem for both partners. A man who has a one-off experience of failure to get an erection or to reach ejaculation may take fright and start believing he'll *never* be able to do it again. The effect of this on some men is that they keep trying until they get there. But, rather more commonly – especially for a man who has suffered a serious blow to his male ego and self-esteem through losing his job – the effect is to put him off sex. Rather than risk failure again, he tends to avoid it. For his partner, there is a rather different reaction.

Most women connect sex with love and affection for their partner. So, if he suddenly goes off sex or seems to be avoiding it or, indeed, tries to have intercourse with her and can't make it, she's quite likely to think that this is because of something *she* has done or not done. She thinks it's *her* fault. She thinks he's gone off her and doesn't find her attractive any more. She thinks she's too fat or too thin or that she's not sexy enough, she's not good enough in bed. Alternatively, she begins to suspect that he's seeing someone else, he's having an affair.

Affairs

Several of the counsellors I talked to mentioned that affairs are a common reaction to an unemployment situation. Affairs generally happen when something else is going on in the relationship. They are almost always a reflection of the relationship between the couple. The third person comes along as a result of, or as a way of resolving, some sort of conflict or situation that has developed in the relationship. When one person is out of work and is spending more time at home than before, there may be new opportunities for meeting someone else and being open to an affair. One counsellor remarked:

> Sometimes an affair becomes just another 'secret' between the couple – something they can't talk about – or something the unemployed one is keeping secret from his partner. It's often symptomatic of the secrecy between them and their inability to be open with each other about their loss and their feelings about it.

An affair may happen not just because he's at home more, but because with someone else he can talk about his feelings without the threat he feels when talking to his wife. The man gains acceptance with the affair that he hasn't got with his family. He can talk and be comforted by the new person. She may only have known him since he's been out of work, whereas the wife knew him when he was in work – perhaps has only known him in work – and to her he's a different man, he's changed.

A male counsellor contributed the thought that:

> Men who need to talk about their redundancy and their feelings about it, will often prefer to talk to a woman. So, if he meets a woman who listens to him, there's a very strong interaction between them from the start, which could lead to an affair. If he bares his soul to another woman, it's a very strong emotional experience. And it's without the

threat of talking to his wife and being seen as less of a person – less of a man – because of exposing his emotions. Perhaps for the first time this woman has seen him cry.

Another counsellor felt that there's often a danger when there is complete role reversal after a redundancy. The woman may become the one who goes out to work every day while the man is left at home with not enough to do. Perhaps there's a neighbour who's at home, too, or he meets someone down at the Jobclub. He may even start looking in a contact magazine.

When there's a terrible loss of self-esteem and a general feeling of rejection – not only by the ex-employer, but, perhaps, also a perceived rejection by the wife, who's busy all day and still doing everything at home – it makes it a very vulnerable time for an affair.

The consensus of opinion from the Northampton counsellors was that affairs springing up at this time can go either way. They can sustain the unemployed person for a time – they're used as a prop while they need it and can then be dropped when they're no longer necessary or when he finds a job – or sometimes they can go on, even replacing the previous, existing relationship.

This book is not intended to be about affairs or about impotence – there are other books dealing with these problems. But, for couples facing up to the difficulties and possible dangers of the new, changed situation and relationship, it's as well to be aware of the things that are sometimes too difficult and threatening to talk about.

How to cope

Talk it out. There's no substitute for talking! If your partner wants much more sex than usual and, after a while, you're beginning to tire or feel like a sex object, raise the subject gently. Suggest, perhaps, that you could make love in other ways rather than constant, daily or more frequent intercourse – penetrative sex. You might get a book from the library about sensual massage and plan a mutual session with aromatherapy oils. The massage could lead to orgasm for both or one, but it wouldn't have to.

You could go back to basics and make love *without* having intercourse. Practising all the techniques of 'heavy petting' – the sort of lovemaking you did when you were teenagers or before you were married can be fun and bring back memories. You could also think of revising your oral and manual sexual skills to bring each other to orgasm.

You could take turns talking about fantasies. Make them up if you'd rather not bring your most private ones out into the open. Try them out – as long as they're not dangerous or threatening to your partner in any way at all. If, for instance, you've always fantasized about making love outdoors, plan a picnic or trip to the seaside, find a very quiet, private spot somewhere romantic and comfortable and let your imagination take over. If, on the other hand, your fantasy is likely to worry or upset your partner, I'd strongly advise *against* making it a reality. Threesomes, group sex or sex involving bondage or dressing up can all lead to problems – and certainly will if one partner is unwilling and only agrees because they're afraid not to. Sex is, above all things, meant to be enjoyable and preferably fun for both those taking part.

I have often written about affairs in my column in *Bella*. Many of the letters I receive are from woman who have discovered that their husbands have been unfaithful. Despite a previous assumption that if he ever did this to them, they would leave or throw him out immediately, more often than not, the wife realizes she doesn't *want* to let her husband go. It's certainly possible to recover from an affair and millions of relationships have gone on to survive afterwards, but it needs considerable understanding of what was behind the affair in the first place and a great deal of effort on both sides to put matters right, put the affair behind them and go on forward.

I would certainly recommend that a couple wanting to work through and recover after an affair, on one or both sides, goes along to a branch of Relate or another local counselling service and asks for help from the counsellors there. It often takes someone else, who's trained to help you see what you're saying and doing with a new objectivity and insight, to offer you a way out of what seems like an irrecoverable situation. Again, it's a matter of teamwork!

For even the most practised team, after a redundancy, there are likely to be sticky patches to go through and, from time to time, both will feel like giving up. Don't do that before you've tried every way you can to get back together.

3
The children

Your children are bound to be affected by the changes in the family and in the household, both emotionally and financially. They'll know something is going on, even if they're very young – children aren't stupid! In fact, I often think they're much more aware and sometimes more sensitive than many parents!

So, even if your instinct is to think they shouldn't know the truth because you want to protect them from worrying, it is better to involve them in the family situation at some level. It is a way of helping them understand what's going on without frightening them unnecessarily and a worthwhile life-training experience for their own future. Not telling them because you're ashamed or feel embarrassed about losing your job is understandable, but unwise. You need their support and encouragement as much as anyone else's.

Avoiding problems

'The children can and do lose out', said a counsellor at Northampton. When the income coming into the household is drastically reduced or even cut by half, there are bound to be unavoidable effects on the whole family. Counsellors say that parents do everything they can to keep the worst effects of redundancy or long-term unemployment from their children, but what upsets them most of all is having to decide what the children can still do or not do, have or go without. But it's essential to be honest and up-front with your children and, indeed, make them part of the family team working to overcome this stormy patch.

Children who are not told the truth about anxieties and stress in the family often try to work out why things they can see and hear are happening and the reasons they come up with might be a great deal worse than the reality. They can even blame themselves for their parents' stress and tension and feel guilty without knowing why. So, you need to talk to your children, at a level they can understand.

Wendy's youngest daughter had just been offered a place at the Royal Ballet School, when her father lost his job. Her first thought was that she wouldn't be able to take it up or even continue to go to ballet classes. Colin and Wendy told their children what had happened straight away:

On the first day, the children all panicked that whatever they do after school would all just come to a halt. But, I explained that it was all paid for up until the end of term at least and we'd sort it all out.

If, when the household financial situation is being looked at in the early days and weeks, money is seriously tight and the children's extra lessons and activities are seen as 'luxuries', the children themselves might be asked to consider what they would be prepared to give up, for a short time, in the interests of the family. In fact, it could be seen as an exercise in 'life management' – budgeting and deciding what is essential and what can be waited for or done without.

Lessons to be learned

Children are essentially selfish – although, of course, adults retain such self-interest in the 'child' that remains within us throughout our lives. So, a child's first reaction to any news of a change in the family is likely to be 'How will it affect me?'

You can help your children by explaining the changed situation as far as possible and, depending on their age, including them in the planning and rethinking and reassessing that must go on in the first days and weeks after the news of the redundancy. Wendy and Colin felt that, in the first few months after Colin lost his job, the children had learned important lessons. Wendy thinks:

> They've learned that you can't always have what you want when you want it, and they understand that if the packets of crisps in the cupboard have run out, they have to wait until the next week's shop for some more. They can't just run to the corner shop.

Colin felt his eldest son had had a 'real jolt'. Colin had had quite a heart-to-heart with him and he felt he'd been able to get through to his son that you can't just 'swan through life'. Colin said he thought his son had realized that he'd got to be a lot more serious about school and qualifications.

If losing my job let him see that life's uncertain and that you've got to be flexible, take up opportunities and never be complacent, that's a good lesson to learn, isn't it?

Colin and Wendy's family is the kind that has no problems in talking with each other, all the time, about everything. So, they expected to discuss the problem of Dad's sudden loss of income with their children and the children expected to be included. If a family is not in the habit of being open like this and there is an existing tension between the parents, the situation can be very different.

THE CHILDREN

Mike and Joyce

Mike and Joyce had been going through a very rocky patch in their marriage for some years before Mike was made redundant. They found it very difficult to talk about almost anything without a row developing, so an uncomfortable level of necessary communication had been established, which coped with ordinary family business and got them by.

Their children were undoubtedly aware of this, but found it easier to get on with their lives and spend as little time in the house with their parents as possible.

Mike had been brought up in a poor family and felt his childhood had been deprived. As a young man, he'd struggled on very low pay, but had studied, gained qualifications and gradually climbed up the ladder until he'd moved over into management.

By his late thirties, he was earning more than he'd ever earned before and he wanted to show it off. Their house was equipped with every new gadget and state-of-the-art domestic appliances.

Mike, like many adults who've felt deprived as children, wanted to give his own children everything – and did. There was a TV in almost every room, they had a computer before anyone else in the street and were given electric guitars and keyboards, skateboards and mountain bikes almost before they asked for them.

When Mike was made redundant, his sense of rejection and shame was so great that he sank into depression. He could not talk about it with Joyce, whom he saw as unsupportive and unhelpful, and he certainly felt unable to talk to his children.

Because he'd fought for and won a very favourable severance payment, he was determined his family would not suffer in material terms. They didn't, but the silence and lack of honesty between them only increased.

In other families, a job loss can act as a real jolt that can change the way the family operates and bring it much more together as a team.

Angry reactions

Colin and Wendy's children were very supportive of their Dad. 'Supportive isn't a word you associate with children', thought Wendy, but they had been very defensive regarding him. They'd also been very angry at the company that had sacked him. They were angry at the people who'd hurt him so much. They'd be angry in the same sort of way if a friend of theirs was being hurt or somebody was hurting their brother or sister. Wendy remembered:

The littlest one wrote a really quite angry note that he was going to send off to Daddy's boss and his sister helped him with the spelling.

They calmed down after a few days, but for some time they were furious if someone from the company telephoned. 'We don't want that horrible man phoning here!', they said.

At the same time, Wendy felt that the children had 'turned on the love', for their father:

> That sounds false, but it wasn't that way. I think they sensed that he needed more love and were there to give as much as they could. They were more cuddly with him.

She felt the children were generally more considerate and more thoughtful than before the redundancy.

Opposite reactions

Some children seem to react very badly. A Northampton counsellor told of a couple who came to Relate because, after months of unemployment, they were being plagued by their children. They were saying to their dad, 'If you were a real Dad, you wouldn't be sitting around at home . . . you'd be able to do this . . . give us the other.' The couple seemed to be coping quite well, but came for help to cope with their children.

These children, and others who react in this way, might be suffering outside the home. Perhaps it happens less now – as redundancy can happen in any family, at any level and in any circumstances – but this was a little while ago, and these children were apparently being taunted at school.

If you're the one child in the class who can't go on school outings or do out-of-school things, like football, skating, music or dancing, or feels it's shameful to be one of the few who has to have free lunches, then it's likely you'll feel hurt and angry and want to blame someone. You can blame your dad because he's lost his job and be angry with him.

But if your dad, and mum, too, can explain from the start that the job was lost through no fault of their own and that the family needs to hold together until something new can be found, there's more of a chance that a reasonable child can be persuaded to cooperate. In fact, if children feel they're being treated as equal members of the family team, they're much more likely to *want* to join in.

Changes

Children don't like change – or, at least, most children don't. Part of the purpose of having parents and family is the safety and stability they provide and surround you with. The knowledge and awareness of things being the same that this brings to children as they grow up are the basic framework for their adult security. If, suddenly, dad, or mum, changes from the person they thought they knew and, overnight, because they've lost their job, becomes a different person – a sad, miserable, moping, depressed person sitting around at home all day – children, understandably, find this frightening. A common response to fear is anger.

Thus, if a child seems to be showing anger towards their parents, they are really saying, 'I don't understand, why aren't you like you used to be? I don't like it!'

Teresa

Teresa's father was made redundant when the small business he worked for went into liquidation. 'He just couldn't cope,' she remembers. 'When I came home from school that day, he looked shrivelled and was completely withdrawn. I felt a great sense of pity for him, which was completely different from the close admiration I'd always had for my Dad.

Her mother and two brothers all rallied round and did their best to help their father, but his sense of failure and rejection was so overwhelming that he became seriously depressed.

Teresa's mother went back to full-time work and also found a nightshift job. Teresa and her older brother got evening, shelf-stacking jobs in a supermarket. But no one could come to terms with the change in their father. He had lost *himself* when he had lost his job – which was the only one he'd ever had since he left school at 16 – and Teresa realizes now that he probably had a breakdown, which went totally unadmitted and unaccepted in the family.

His personality changed and, without being conscious of what was happening to them at the time, the family broke up around him.

Teresa is still angry at her father and has now lost contact with him. When she married, last year, she didn't even tell him. She thinks of him as if he has died.

She resents the loss of the man she looked up to and respected. She feels angry for the way he treated her mother and, most of all, she mourns the loss of her childhood memories of her strong, funny, patient and comforting dad.

I feel sad about Teresa's story. Sad that a family broke up after a redundancy, but mostly saddened that this could probably have been prevented, or at least certainly have been handled better, especially if Teresa's father had been helped and treated for his depression and her mother and the children could have been helped to understand it.

Depression is a major problem after redundancy and this is tackled in more detail in Chapter 7.

Anger is all around, too, and it's much better if it's got out of the system – expressed, if you like – rather than repressed or hidden.

'Don't tell Dad you're feeling angry or really upset that you went to the shop and didn't have enough money to buy a can of Coke, because that will upset him.' Northampton counsellors have found that this is the sort of remark that children and the other partner will say about the one who's out of work.

> The redundant person is seen as the one who's in need – the one who needs looking after. So, everyone goes along, hiding their *own* needs and their frustrations, and they become less themselves and less true to themselves. Then there's a general lack of family intimacy – a closing down in the family – it's like putting a lid on it.

What happens is that, being treated this way, leads to isolation in the family. A counsellor who works with the families of alcoholics finds the situations comparable:

> All the focus is on the alcoholic. The rest of the family are creeping around, frightened to death to upset him or her. It's a protection racket.

And it doesn't, in the end, help the one with the problem, whether it's alcoholism or redundancy.

Feeling isolated is common enough anyway for someone who is suffering from the terrible feeling of rejection by an employer and by the working world. He or she needs to feel part of what's going on around them, and, being out, being with people and talking to them, whoever it is, is part of the survival strategy. The feelings of anger, too, need to be talked about, by all members of the family, however hard it feels to do this. It's a mistake to bottle it up. Again, this is dealt with in more detail in Chapter 7.

Involving the children

Peter Trigg, Managing Director of international human resource consultancy Drake Beam Morin in London, has put together some hints and tips for parents living with redundancy. He's convinced that children need to be told the truth about their parent's loss of job so they don't imagine a situation that is worse than the reality. Telling your child that the job you used to do at that company, factory or whatever, is no longer necessary and you have to find another is clear and simple to understand. It may reassure the child, as well as perhaps boosting the morale of the parent, to explain that losing the job wasn't a reflection of how well you'd been doing it or how good a person you were.

It's helpful to reassure your children, too, that you only intend this situation to be a temporary one, but that the whole family needs to work together to get through this difficult time. Children do like to be asked to help and some might enjoy the idea of working out how to cut down on unnecessary family expenditure. It could even be used as a maths project!

If your children want to ask questions about what's happened or what might happen in the future, let them do it in their own time. They might well want to come back to a subject you thought you'd covered – like whether or not you'll have a holiday this year or if they'll be able to go on the school trip – but it's important they feel they're free to ask you about it.

Try to keep as calm and undefensive about their concerns, when they voice them, as you can – however upset and worried you feel inside.

Depending on their age, give them things to do so they feel part of the team. Being responsible for fetching the local paper from the newsagent each week or helping choose the right tie or outfit for an interview, is something they can be involved with, if they want to be. Don't press it if they don't!

If major changes in the family seem to be a real possibility – like moving house or changing schools – try to encourage a positive attitude to this, but don't alarm the children unnecessarily, mentioning them *before* they become a real likelihood.

Training children to use the telephone

Peter Trigg and another consultant, Michael Witcher, in another interview, mentioned the importance of training the older children in the family to answer the telephone sensibly and efficiently.

If you've sent off an application form or written on spec to a company, let the children know. Fix a list of the people and companies you've approached, who might call, by the telephone, so whoever answers the call will respond properly and if you're not there, answer well and take a message efficiently.

If a Personnel Manager or a Director of a company telephones your home as a result of your approach and is met with a careless, sulky or rude-sounding voice, he or she might be forgiven for putting a mental cross against your name or, worse, not bothering to pursue the matter! Handling telephone calls in a businesslike manner is useful training for any child anyway, but can make all the difference in these circumstances.

If you're successful in being given an interview, ask the children's advice and help in choosing the best outfit to wear. If nothing else, children tell the truth about how you look, what suits you and what doesn't look good!

Remaining positive

It'll help you, the parents, and, at the same time, reassure the children if you try to maintain as positive and hopeful an outlook on the job search as possible.

Finding opportunities for as many family outings or treats as can be managed helps children feel that things haven't changed or are not changing too drastically. Indeed, having mum or dad around more can be seen as a positive benefit!

'Spending more time with my family' is a well-worn politician's excuse for leaving office, but, in fact, this is exactly what many parents do when they are forced to be at home because they're out of work. People, especially men, who've been concentrating in a desperate, driven way on a competitive career and have had to stop and think when they lose their job, often report a new appreciation of life and the people around them. They may realize, with a sense of shock or even shame, that previously they've almost taken the children and their partner for granted.

Peter Trigg makes the point that it's wise and sensible to try to make sure that your children see that you are in control of this situation, however worrying it may be for everyone. Children need to believe, for as long as possible, that their parents are 'all powerful', that they can make things happen, look after them and take care of them when things go wrong. Later on, as they grow up and go through adolescence, they have to break away and be responsible for looking after themselves, but it is best if they do that then rather than at a young age. They learn about what being 'grown up' – being an adult – means from the adults around them when they're children, and they can learn all sorts of useful or essential lessons from your redundancy. At worst, they can learn that life and work are unpredictable and skills, determination and adaptability are necessary in order to survive. At best, they can learn about facing up to and coping with difficulties, solving problems and working as a team. These are lessons that will stand them in very good stead for the rest of their lives.

4
How the other half feels

After the initial shock, experiences of dismay, sympathy for the feelings of the partner who's been treated so badly and so on, the 'other half' of the couple will start to think and worry about how the redundancy will affect their life.

If it's a completely new situation, it will all seem strange and frightening. You will feel lost and unable to know where to begin. Wendy said.

> Thoughts were going through my head so fast. What do we do first? What happens now? What do I cut out? Where do I begin?

First thoughts – money

Money is usually the first concern. There's an instant reaction to cut things out and cut down on expenditure – a feeling of needing to pull in the belt and spend less without at first knowing what that will mean in real terms.

For many there will be a redundancy payment or, more euphemistically, a severance payment, which may feel like a lot of money or not very much at all when suddenly the future is so uncertain.

Dealing with money

How money is dealt with in relationships varies enormously. For some couples, the traditional pattern of the man bringing home the wage packet each Friday night to hand over to the woman to sort out is still maintained. Many women who write to me do see themselves, and are seen as, the money manager – the holder of the purse strings. For others, the man comes home with the pay and hands over the housekeeping to the woman, keeping the rest firmly for himself. They may have worked out and agreed a weekly budget together or he may feel it's his role to manage the money for his family and she accepts this because this is also her experience of how families are run. Indeed, for many women, the man's earnings are a mystery, a closed book that they either aren't allowed to know about or do not feel the need to know about.

A Relate counsellor told me of the wife who had been abandoned by her husband – he had lost his job and, shortly afterwards, run away. She was in her early fifties and she had never in her life had to pay a bill or write a cheque. Her husband had done everything for her and she had been content to let him do so because he was the 'manager' in their relationship.

While being helped to go through her distress at the loss of her husband, she also had to be shown how to use a chequebook. She was, the counsellor felt, like a wife from the 1930s being forced to come to terms with managing life in the 1990s.

This was the beginning of a new phase in her life, which she hadn't anticipated and was seriously ill-equipped to deal with. But, apparently, after the initial shock and sadness, she took to it all like a duck to water.

If the financial system in the family – whatever it is – has worked until now, this may be the time when you will need a whole new system of management – a new way of approaching money. There's a definite need for discussion, careful thought and planning. Achieving mutual agreement on how the resources should be shared out and spent is much to be recommended. If this is a new way of running the household for you, this will be perhaps the first major adjustment you will make.

Upsetting the balance

I remember reading a book entitled *Making Marriage Work* (by Dr Paul Hauck, now out of print) in which it was recommended that a couple getting married should look on their marriage as if they were managing a business partnership. That is, that it has to be a business which is shared equally, or as equally as possible, and which both parties can feel is of benefit to them.

There will inevitably be problems if one partner feels there is an unfair imbalance in benefits or of contributions. So, when existing 'balances' are turned upside down because of the loss of a job, the new dynamics of the relationship and the partnership have to be reassesed and, perhaps, renegotiated. Doing this requires a high degree of tolerance and understanding on both sides, but, perhaps, more from the partner who has *not* been made redundant. However, they may well feel that they're having to make these new adjustments through no fault of their own and as a result of a situation over which they have no control. It's this 'out of control' feeling that can lead to resentments, which may – however deeply hidden or unacknowledged they are – cause problems for the couple.

Space invaders

When Sylvia wrote to me, she was feeling anxious, uncertain of how things would be for her and the family, now that Dad was no longer going out to work at the mine. She wrote as she would have spoken – as many of us do when we're writing about feelings – so I could vividly imagine the anxious, almost embarrassed, laugh at the end of the sentence – '. . . we will both be in the house together most of the time (help!) ha! ha!'

As she wrote she was clearly thinking that it would be a worry, even tiresome and irritating, to have her husband, much as she loved him, around the house during the day when, probably, for the entire time they'd been together, he'd gone out of the house first thing during the week and come home for his tea. She seems to have been feeling almost embarrassed to be thinking this way, hence the bracketed 'help'.

This issue of space in a relationship is extremely important and there are many elements to it. However close and warm the friendship and companionship between the couple, there is generally a need for time to yourself – a little solitude – when you can do whatever you have to do, or want to do, in the way you want to do it without the other person's involvement. You may choose to tell your partner what you've done in that space at the end of the day, if that's the kind of relationship you have, or you may see it as a part of the day that's your business and has little or nothing to do with them. In some ways it's private time. So, the idea of giving up this space and time or having to share it and manage it differently can seem to present a problem.

For some couples, the time apart during the day has been taken for granted. It's only when this is lost and they find themselves together all day and every day that their need to be apart becomes clear. These couples are often afraid of being too close together, afraid of real 'intimacy' – a word that came up often when talking with Relate counsellors. They have become dependent on the separation during the day they've always known. They know how to handle this. This space apart gives them a chance to prepare for the return of the other, but they don't know how to live together all the time. It's not only the time to yourself that is lost or threatened. There's a very real danger that the one who's lost their job thinks that one way of filling their time would be to take over some or all of the running of the household.

A man who's been used to managing may imagine that he could manage the household and 'help' his partner, who has probably had sole charge of this role throughout their relationship. There are stories of men who have retired or been made redundant from the armed forces who leap at the chance of running their house and garden and social life as if it were an army platoon. One man who'd been a colonel set about completely reorganizing the house, rearranging all the cupboards, making endless lists, labelling shelves, issuing 'daily orders', which he pinned up on the kitchen door, but omitting to assign anything much for his wife to do. As a consequence, she too felt 'redundant' and her reaction to this was to sink into inactivity and illness, which became serious depression.

Feeling angry and defensive on your partner's behalf

Vicky said when John rang her at work to tell her he'd just been 'let go':

> I was shocked and furiously angry. I was so angry with Richard, John's boss. I was ranting and raving and I rang John back and told him to put me on to Richard. I wanted to tell him myself how angry I was. He was a sort of friend and he'd been to our wedding. John of course said, 'You can't do that'.
>
> I was still angry a couple of days later but, instead of being angry at the person who'd sacked John, I started taking it out on John. I was very bossy with him – telling him what to do and asking him what he'd done to get a job all the time. I wanted him to get on and get a new job and John's very laid back – he needs a bit of a push.
>
> I was telling my Mum about it and she said she was ashamed of me and how I was behaving, which made me think.
>
> John's usually very even-tempered, but, a few nights later when I came home from work, I was asking him what he'd done and who'd he'd taken his CV to and he just said, 'Vicky – give me a break!' I burst into tears and said I was sorry I was being so horrid. I felt so sorry for him. I didn't want to see him more rejected. I felt angry and protective, too.

Sympathetic anger is a very common reaction for partners at first. Dealing with their partner's anger is another issue. On that first afternoon when he came home with his redundancy letter and cheque, you will recall that Wendy's husband, Colin, snapped at her when she raised her voice and told him he always walked away when they were having a serious discussion and said, 'Don't you start getting at me – I nearly put the car through a brick wall on the way home, I can tell you!' Wendy said:

> I've really got to watch what I say to him. No matter what I feel, I can't *say* what I feel because I don't want to upset him more than necessary. So, for the next few days, I had to watch what I said and I didn't ask too many questions. It wasn't for about a week that I heard some of the answers and got the full story. I don't know whether he didn't want to talk about it or didn't think I was interested, didn't

think it concerned me or didn't want to worry me. It wasn't until we went to talk to a friend who's a personnel manager for a firm of accountants that I heard the full story of how he was sacked. Now I want to write to the company and ask them all sorts of questions.

It's helped me that we've had so many phone calls from Colin's customers. None of them have been informed, so we've had lots of calls from customers who knew his home phone was a good way of getting a message to him. They're just shattered. I've had to be a bit careful with customers and said, 'Did you know Colin isn't with A... any longer?' If they haven't heard, they're shattered and if they have, they've often rung because they wanted to say how awful they think it was and they wanted to wish him all the best. That made Colin feel really good, the fact that people are so shocked and feel it's an unjustified step. You can't say 'It's not fair' about work, can you, but they say they can't understand the logic of taking salespeople off the road when you're still trying to sell a product. That's been very good and supportive.

Giving more loving

In the first few days, Wendy said she felt she had to give Colin a lot more love:

> You need to say you still need him and love him. I think the female partner has to be very supportive – to make a conscious effort not to say anything or do anything that could be too questioning – he's had enough criticism.

I asked if she thought Colin had appreciated her support and her loving.

> He doesn't say – he never does. I don't think he said to himself, 'She seems to want a lot more love than she normally does.' It might have gone through his head, but he certainly hasn't declared himself.

The initial, supportive and defensive reaction can often change over the next few days and weeks. Vicky found herself getting irritable with John, partly because she was afraid that his being out of work would affect their life together, but also because it occurred to her that it might affect her own life:

> I didn't want to feel resentful that he wasn't going out to work and I was. And I didn't want him to resent me working and enjoying my

job. I was worried it was going to have an effect on our social life. I didn't think I'd be able to come home and talk about what was going on for me at work. And I worried that I wouldn't be able to go out for a drink after work without worrying about getting home to John.

Vicky was able to be brutally honest about her own reactions, which she described as selfish. At the time, though, she found all sorts of worries were occupying her mind that she felt ashamed of, but which were genuine and valid:

> We were living in the flat John had before we married and I hated the part of town it was in. I desperately wanted to move out and we'd been looking around. Now he was out of work, I was worried we would never be able to move away without two salaries.

Viv said that she soon started to resent being the breadwinner when her husband, Phil, lost his highly paid job with a firm of consultants. Viv was earning good money herself, but, until then, she'd been able to spend a lot of it on herself.

> I spent a lot of money on clothes, we had two foreign holidays a year and two cars. Phil was Chairman of the local Round Table and I had a busy social life with the Ladies Circle. But, without Phil's income, most of our savings went on the mortgage and living expenses. My salary couldn't cover it all.
>
> I know I was in the wrong sometimes. I was critical and should have been more tolerant. I used to come home from work and ask him what he'd done to get a job. It would all blow up into an argument. I resented the fact he could spend all day doing what he liked while I was working.
>
> I felt there was a wall building up around Phil and I just couldn't get through it. Phil suffered a lot of self-doubt and I felt he had no urge to find another job.

Eighteen months after Phil became unemployed, Viv's own job was lost when her company carried out a major restructuring exercise. A year later, Viv and Phil were divorced. Money had been what had brought this couple together. They both enjoyed it and, when they'd met, they'd both been earning good salaries. They enjoyed an expensive lifestyle, to which they both felt they contributed equally. However, when one stopped contributing, the other soon found a bitter resentment building up that neither of them could handle. They drifted further and further apart and, despite Viv going along to Relate on her own (I wasn't told why Phil did not or would not go), the marriage ended in bitterness and acrimony. It was the second marriage for them both, which may be relevant.

After six months, Wendy's support for Colin was wearing a bit thin.

> Things do begin to get on top of you after a while. Colin's like a walking zombie. He doesn't do anything. Friends of ours have asked him, 'Where's your old get up and go?' and he just says, 'It got up and went.'
>
> I'm not noted as a patient person – I admit it. I like to be in control of my part of life, my own situation.
>
> I suppose Colin's depressed. He feels he's not much good for any other job. I've suggested jobs that I've seen in the paper and which seem to me to be really up his street, but he won't even apply.

There's a note of irritation in Wendy's voice that wasn't there at the beginning – this is a dangerous time.

They're thinking of swapping roles – Wendy going back to full-time work and Colin leaving the job he's come to hate so much and taking over the management of the B&B business. But Wendy isn't sure it's the right thing to do, for either of them:

> He wouldn't be getting dressed in a suit and putting on a tie to go to work every day. It's not his own thing – it's not challenging, it's not getting out and meeting different people every day and being his own boss. I'm afraid it might further lower his self-esteem. I don't know whether it would give him a worthwhile feeling of usefulness in life.

The partner's reaction can be a reaction to loss, in conjunction with the loss the unemployed person is feeling.

Compulsory retirement

In some ways, the sudden change from one partner going out to work every day, to them being around 'under your feet' all the time, is comparable with retirement.

Nowadays, there are courses that people who are approaching retirement age can go on or which are provided by their employers – as well as books to read – that aim to help both partners cope with this commonly accepted life change. As with most major crossroads in life, those who cope best are those who are better prepared and, by nature, more adaptable or versatile. A friend of mine confided when her husband first retired, 'I couldn't believe he wants to come to the supermarket with me.' Her husband had had a long and successful career, commuting to London from their rural home, while she managed the house, the children and a variety of part-time jobs, as well as doing voluntary work she thoroughly enjoyed. Neither of them had given any thought to his retirement and what it would mean to their lives, so it came as a bit of a shock to realize that not only would they be together 24 hours a day, but that this would not be an entirely enjoyable experience!

My friend is of a rather fiery, excitable nature, but, fortunately, her husband is one of the most calm, even-tempered laid back men I've ever known. After long years of experience in the give and take of marriage, they were able to find their own ways of adjusting to their new lifestyle. Each maintains some time in the week when they do their own thing, but they've also taken advantage of the fact that they have more time for doing the things they enjoy together.

Retirement is like when one partner has lost their job in terms of the change of balance in the relationship and the adjustments that need to be made in the management of the time they're suddenly forced to share together. It can also be comparable in terms of loss. Retirement brings a sometimes unexpected feeling of loss – of status, the company of colleagues, a social life away from the home and perhaps also, of course, the loss of income.

For the partner there can be a comparable feeling of loss of status. You're no longer the partner of a manager, sales executive, supervisor, police officer, firefighter or whatever, but the partner of a formerly employed person – someone who is retired.

The main and most crucial difference between retirement and redundancy, however, is that the retirement is not, generally, forced whereas redundancy is.

A bereavement

Losing your job has also often been compared with losing a loved one through death. Certainly, the emotional reactions to the loss in both these situations are similar. Very early on in my counselling training, a counsellor described the stages of grief as being:

- mad
- bad
- sad
- glad.

This is obviously an extremely simplified version of the process of mourning and, of course, people don't always follow patterns rigidly, but, still, it is an easy way of thinking about the process of loss.

At first – when your partner is made redundant – you feel angry, hurt and rail against the unfairness of the employer, the Government, the world and the universe.

This first reaction often leads straight into, or exists alongside, the terrible feelings of rejection – one of the most powerful and painful of emotions. As the partner, you may feel angry and defensive because this person you love has been hurt.

The feelings that follow these are sometimes 'bad' in the sense that you may find yourself wondering why your partner lost their job. What did they do that they were sacked? Why didn't they see it coming? Why was it them and not someone else? Quite soon, there could be feelings of anger with your partner, for putting you and the family through all this: 'How could they do this to me?'

After a bereavement, there's a danger of becoming stuck in these 'bad' feelings, of being unable to move on or climb out of them. This can lead to serious depression, so it's important to be aware that these stages need to be moved *through* in order to maintain some degree of reality or even sanity.

After the turmoil of these destructive emotions, a more peaceful and accepting sadness for the love, friendship and companionship that has been lost can develop, which, in bereavement, over time, can turn into an acceptance and understanding that the loved one will always be there in memories. Perhaps the comparison between bereavement and redundancy becomes rather less close here, but an awareness of the feelings that are commonly experienced and, indeed, have to be struggled through as a result of almost any major loss in life, can be helpful. You've started on a major process of change in your lives and in your relationship and there are changes ahead that cannot be avoided.

Who knows what's right for the other?

Wendy seems to be worrying about Colin and whether he'll be happy in what has been, up to now, her role as household manager and manager of the B&B business. But, does she see the job she's been doing for six years as unchallenging? It's been good enough for her, it's paid the mortgage and allowed her to be at home for the children before and after school. Why would it not be good enough for Colin in the meantime? Wouldn't it be better than him going off every working day to a job he hates, one that is making him increasingly depressed and apathetic?

There's a danger – when a couple have been together for some while – for the established patterns to become rigid and for it to become frightening to think of them altering or for there to be a change in roles. Is Wendy stuck with an image of how she thinks Colin *ought* to be or what he *should* be doing for a living? Does she think he would be less of a man if he took over her job at home? Is she afraid she would lose respect for him if he did?

Asking the questions

Being out of work changes everything for the family. Because this new situation has so dramatically altered the status quo in your life, relationship and family, it's absolutely essential, if you want it to hold together, to ask some important questions about yourself and about the relationship.

How do you see the male and female roles? For example, if you're honest, do you believe that the man should be the breadwinner? Do you think there are some jobs that are suitable for a man and some that are beneath him? Do you believe the woman is the only one who can run the home properly? Do you feel anxious, worried or resentful about sharing the daytime hours with your partner? Do you feel afraid your position in the home and in the family will be challenged or eroded?

These are just some of the questions that you would do well to consider and discuss, where appropriate, together.

Points to ponder

What roles do you and your partner play in your relationship or what roles did you play before the unemployment? Are you sticking rigidly to the same roles or are you ready and willing to adjust and adapt?

Relate counsellors, who've worked with many hundreds of couples whose lives have been changed as a result of redundancy and unemployment, and outplacement counsellors – the term for counsellors who are paid by companies making staff cuts or restructuring to help individuals and their partners deal with the damage the company has caused – have all become convinced that people and couples who manage unemployment best are those who can be sufficiently unselfish and generous to let go of their pre-existing roles in the relationship and renegotiate a different balance.

Before you can let it go, though, you have to know what role you believed you held! So, the first step is to think that through.

The role we take on in a relationship is incredibly important, but, quite often, we don't *know* what role we're actually playing until we're forced to look at it because we've lost it or it's changed. At such crisis points, it's useful to look at your relationship and see what role each of you plays. Some typical pairings might be the following.

- *Master–servant* One gives the instructions while the other sees their

role as that of 'doing what I'm told'. The 'servant' is often happy to take this role because it absolves them of responsibility. Like members of the armed forces, they are trained to obey commands.
- *Parent–child* One takes care of the other and 'knows best' when decisions need to be made.
- *Active–passive* One does all the 'doing' while the other does just enough but no more. The 'doer' often complains that they're run off their feet but secretly believes that only they can do everything properly.
- *Aggressor–pacifier* One is seen as having a short fuse and a volatile temperament while the other is constantly careful to mollify and pacify.

In many relationships, each partner colludes with the other in maintaining the perceived roles because this is what they know and feel safe with. Thus, if one of them changes role, slips out of it a little or gives it up completely, the other may be quite unable to come to terms with the changes this means for their own role, which, of course, they have lost at the same time. So, for example, although Wendy found running the house as a B&B stressful and was considering going back to a full-time job outside the home, she felt reluctant to allow Colin to take it on instead of doing the job he didn't like because she feared he wouldn't do it properly:

> I suppose he could learn to cook a breakfast, but, at the moment, he burns water. I can't see him making beds and he'd never see the skirting boards need washing down – I can't understand how he can just sit in front of the telly when there's so many things that need doing.

A woman who'd been seen by her partner as 'strong and successful' changed when she was made redundant the first time and became, as she said, 'this crying little thing who wanted to be taken care of'. He couldn't cope with this and left, so then she was dealing with both the loss of her job and the loss of her partner.

A counsellor told of another couple who worked for the same company, but in different departments, and were living together on two average salaries. When he gave in his notice to take up the offer of a job overseas, they were planning for a rosy future, with a big salary coming in from his side. Unfortunately, the Gulf War put an end to his new job, but it was too late for him to retract his notice. So he was suddenly out of work.

He sank into depression and she found it impossible to cope with him sitting at home moping and feeling sorry for himself. She'd also lost the pleasure she'd taken in being with him when he had money and the loss of status in front of their friends. She was suddenly the 'provider' and, on her income, suddenly money was extremely tight. The relationship broke down under the strain.

Teamwork

The key to your surviving all this, as a couple, is, as before, teamwork. You have to be prepared to communicate. You have to talk through all these feelings in a fair and honest way in order to navigate your way through all the major sea changes without disaster.

5
Taking stock

Michael's view

For many men their jobs are evidence of what they are on the outside and how they see themselves from the inside. They're the outward statement of our positions in the community. How often in a social situation, when meeting for the first time, do people say to each other, 'What do you do?' What they're really saying is, 'Tell me your position in our society.'

For most men, their jobs define what sort of men they are. Their jobs also define how successful they have been. Women, on the other hand, when meeting each other for the first time, are more likely to ask something much more personal, such as 'Have you lived in this area for long?' or ask about children – how many and how old they are.

For an unemployed man – especially a relatively newly out of work one – the instinctive reaction is to become defensive. And one of the many effects of his crushing loss of confidence is the feeling that the employed person is adopting a superior attitude to him. The reality is probably that the employed man feels so threatened by the idea of redundancy himself that he, in turn, becomes defensive.

Although we try to put a brave face on being out of work, nothing can actually compensate for the loss of self-esteem that comes from losing your position in the pecking order. We're no longer a miner, salesperson, bank clerk, departmental manager or company director, we're a *former* whatever it was – an unemployed person. We may not have a car or a pension or private health insurance or any of the other things we once took for granted. We are no longer paid, we're dependent on welfare benefits. Even those who are fortunate enough to receive some cash settlement – redundancy or severance pay – must remember to sign on in order to ensure that State retirement benefits are not affected. In such an uncertain world, there's no guarantee of finding a new job that will provide a company pension scheme. It's bad enough to be without work – it will be worse to be without a pension. Certainly, signing on can be a traumatic experience for those who have never previously had to do it.

Take a deep breath

We're often told to take a deep breath when faced with any stressful situation. This one is no different. 'Stand still', as it were, for a moment and think. Don't make a resolution to live on bread and water from now on before you've properly considered everything that this entails.

TAKING STOCK

Reg and Joan

Reg and Joan sat up all night after Reg was made redundant, carefully calculating how little they could live on. Every item of expenditure was considered – right down to the price of the daily newspapers. The next morning, Reg was at the newsagent's at 7.30 am to cancel his order, but, three days later, he was back. He'd forgotten that newspapers are an excellent source of job advertisements! Happily for Reg and Joan, with their family up and grown, they were able to survive on Joan's income until Reg found another job.

Start by making lists

It is wise to do as Reg and Joan did, writing down everything that you spend as a household and then adding the things you'll need to help you find another job. Your job now is finding *another* job.

Essential expenditure includes:

- food
- clothing
- mortgage or rent
- loans and credit card payments
- maintenance payments
- education
- Council Tax
- electricity
- gas
- water
- telephone
- television licence, cable, satellite
- car
- transport
- subscriptions
- and so on.

Economies

Although it may not seem like it, there are a few financial advantages that go with being unemployed. You won't have to buy a season ticket or spend as much on petrol as if you had to travel to work. You won't need your work clothes laundered or your business suits cleaned. You won't have to buy snacks or lunches out or pick up your round of drinks in the pub for colleagues. If it wasn't for the sudden drop in income, you might actually grow to like the new situation!

TAKING STOCK

What do you need?

Once you've worked out what it costs to keep body and soul together, you can start making two more lists:

- one of all the things you're going to need in order to start applying for jobs;
- one of all the people you're going to write to.

It's a brutally competitive world out there. Just because you can do a job doesn't mean that you can rely on that experience in order to walk into another position. There are literally millions of people looking for new employment. Some of them like you, but many of them already in work. You can't disguise the fact you're unemployed and they're not and you can't help the natural reaction of prospective employers, wondering *why* you're unemployed, particularly if you were the only one to have been made redundant.

It doesn't matter whether you want a position on the shop floor or in the boardroom, the first impression you make will be vital in securing an interview. If you're going to make a bad impression, don't waste your time and effort or the price of a stamp. Once you've created the wrong impression, it's extremely difficult, if not impossible, to salvage the situation.

In these days of high technology, there's absolutely no need for anyone to have a badly presented CV. Even if you can't afford your own computer, there are specialist bureaux throughout the country that will prepare a CV relatively inexpensively (see Chapter 7 for further details). If you feel you cannot afford this, then try any friends who have access to a computer or use the Jobclubs, which are set up to provide services and facilities for those who are actively seeking work.

Keep reminding yourself that your job now is to find a new job. If you've received redundancy money or a severance payment, it's probably better to spend it on buying a computer and printer to prepare your new CV than saving it for a rainy day. Unless you've been particularly fortunate and received a six- or seven-figure compensation package, you're going to have to try your absolute hardest to find another position before those rainy days arrive. Also, keyboard skills are an essential part of today's business environment, so you can, at the same time, learn or improve your computing skills, which will help when you find another job.

So, what will you need?

- Good-quality A4 paper (at least 100 gsm bond or laser printer quality).

- Envelopes for A4 (the same colour as the paper, but not necessarily of the same quality – the envelope won't be opened by whoever makes the selection for interview, but that person will be able to tell if the CV was squeezed into one of the wrong size).
- First-class stamps.
- The names and addresses of contacts and companies.

Newspapers, magazines and trade or professional journals are an obvious source but you need to be aware that they're probably being read by between 15,000 and 15,000,000 potential competitors. Somebody has to win, but it can mean betting on a very long shot. Public advertisements often attract an absurdly high degree of competition, which is frequently out of all proportion to the position on offer. The best way to handle these opportunities is to be extremely rigorous in your self-assessment. Measure yourself against the advertised job and person specifications as if you were the employer or the recruitment consultant.

It's usually a good idea to see your application through the eyes of the staff of a recruitment agency. They are, typically, extremely skilled at finding out what an employer wants and then phrasing their requirements appropriately in the advertisement. If it specifies age, experience and qualifications, there is no benefit to them in putting forward a candidate who doesn't meet the agreed specifications. It doesn't matter what *you* may think about your age or what value you place on your particular qualifications or experience – in a competitive job market, you're unlikely even to be considered. You have to be the first judge of your own elegibility, so, if you don't pass that test, don't apply. Save the paper and postage for a more realistic opportunity.

So, what is the best approach? First, use your knowledge and your creative skills. You might think there's not much point in suggesting that, if you're among a thousand others who have lost jobs in shipyards, steel mills or coalmines, you should write to all the other employers in your industry. Once upon a time there were no other employers. Now, of course, there are.

You'll find the names and addresses of these at your local library. There are directories for almost every industry and yearbooks for almost every profession. If your library hasn't got what you're looking for, there's every possibility they'll help you to find it.

Think carefully about what work you did in your previous employment. Pick out the positive parts, skills, responsibilities and so on that could be of interest to other employers, and start writing.

It's been tragic watching the decline of so many steel towns and pit villages, but just as unsettling witnessing the attitude, 'That's what I do.

They don't do that any more. I'll never work again.' It simply isn't true. You may not work in the same way or in the same industry, you may not even receive payment, but you *will* and *must* work if you are to preserve your self-esteem and remain employable.

Such changes in attitude take a long time to work their way through the system, but there is already anecdotal evidence that this is happening in certain sections of society. For example, middle-class kids with unemployed parents are becoming as cynical of white-collar employment prospects as working-class youngsters from those areas that once supported heavy industry are about the prospects of new blue-collar jobs. It doesn't matter who you are or where you're from, if you can't demonstrate that you're a highly motivated self-starter, you won't fit into the current scheme of things.

What have you got to sell?

It may seem obvious, but whether you're applying for a job in your own specialist field or trying to break into a completely new industry, you need to sell your individual skills and past successes in a positive way. If you're one of those negative people who doesn't think you have *any* skills, think again. You've managed to stay alive this long after all! What you really mean is that you've become unaccustomed to either viewing your skills in an objective way or practising them in a different environment. Ask yourself a few questions.

- Am I intelligent?
- Am I articulate?
- Am I punctual?
- Am I hard-working?
- Am I open-minded?
- Am I willing to learn?
- Am I willing to work for less money?

These are all matters that prospective employers will want to consider in every candidate who catches their attention.

Remember that, in the case of a nationally advertised position, there may be over 1,000 applicants, and the initial cull will frequently be undertaken by a clerk, secretary or even the office junior. Indeed, one set of applications was, to my certain knowledge, assessed first by a temporary clerk, a student who'd just arrived from New Zealand! It's amazing how cavalier some companies can be about considering your best efforts at seeking new employment. It's easy simply to instruct a junior staff member to 'pick out all the applications from people under

35 who have a degree'. It is much less easy to monitor, or even to care about, whether or not the task has been done thoroughly.

If you're going to win at this game, you have to know the unpublished rules. It seems highly likely that it won't be long before this sort of trawl is done by optical readers – just programme the computer with a few key words and pass the applications under the scanner. Then, if you didn't have those key words in your application, it would go straight into the shredder! But, back to the present. Read the application form. Answer the questions *honestly*. If you can meet the requirements of the advertised post, then say so in your application.

A useful rule of thumb to apply when evaluating an advertisement is to consider yourself eligible if you meet at least two-thirds of the advertised requirements. Unless the ad is just a procedural device (only ever used in equal opportunities organizations), you can then be reasonably certain that there will be no 'perfect' candidate, so your application will be on a par with many others. This rule *doesn't* apply, of course, if the two points out of six on which you fail are that you're a *man* over *50* and they asked for a *woman* under *30*!

Improving your chances

Try to give yourself 'an unfair advantage'. If you can afford to work more cheaply than other applicants or are prepared to consider a more flexible form of contractual relationship, for example, then say so. Such positive factors in your favour are particularly relevant when age is an issue. If you're over 50, your mortgage is paid off and the children have left home, you have a marketable advantage over the younger applicant with a young family and negative equity, so use it!

You don't have to use such advantages in the employment stakes – you can actually start thinking of the other opportunities that are available to you, particularly if you've worked out exactly what you need in order to get by. Such thinking opens up a whole new world of possibilities. If you only need to earn £100 a week to pay the household bills, why hold out for £500 a week and a car simply because that's what you're used to? Being unemployed is one thing, but using unemployment as a time to re-evaluate your lifestyle is completely different.

Improving your prospects

Over the past 20 years or so, during which time unemployment has become a political football that is kicked about between Government and the Opposition, politicians of all persuasions seem to have adopted a somewhat simplistic approach to the whole idea of being out of work. The only recognized reasons for unemployment are idleness and lack of skill. As a consequence, workfare and training are seen to be the obvious solutions. I suggest that it's not like that at all.

One of the first problems you encounter when you are out of work is that the skills that were your strongest selling point, and which may have taken you years to learn, are now no longer as valuable as you once thought. A frequent first reaction is to tell yourself that it's their loss and they'll be sorry when you start working for the competition. Sadly, unless you happen to be the one cog that exactly fits their corporate wheel, the competition isn't quite thinking that way.

As we said earlier, your *new* job is *finding* a job. The best way of doing that is to make contact with people you know or once knew who are in the same line of business and may be in a position to influence your selection. Your foreman may have got a job as a manager with another company and now has some say in selection and recruitment there, for example. Whether you call it 'networking' or the 'old pals act', it amounts to the same thing. Start by using your personal relationships to find new work.

Sometimes this can seem particularly difficult, especially if you've previously occupied a senior position. It's very hard to swallow your pride and admit to friends and former colleagues that you're out of work, but it's something you have to do.

If you don't like the idea of doing this, accept the basic jobseeker's benefit, just above £45, deduct enough to pay your household running costs, then try to live on the remainder. If you don't want to live like that for the rest of your life, the thought of it may be a useful spur to action.

If the people you contact don't want to help you, it's probably a good indication that things aren't going to be easy and that you should start casting your net far and wide immediately.

Some human resource experts believe that technical ability accounts for only 20 per cent of the qualities that make an individual attractive to employ. We have not researched this area closely, but many of the people we spoke to believed that their technical competence exceeded that of those former colleagues who escaped redundancy. The obvious conclusion must be that if you're a personable individual with an adequate comprehension of the work you're expected and employed to do, then you'll survive in the job longer than will more expert but 'difficult' people. This has to be borne in mind when you're applying for new jobs. If you've been made redundant, prospective employers will want to know the real reasons for this. Although it is ostensibly the post and not the individual that has been made redundant, the reality is most often very different. Non-conformists rarely stabilize organizations.

Coming to terms with the possibility that your strengths are not the best entrée to another job can be quite unsettling, particularly if you've achieved a level of responsibility within an organization.

Keith

Keith was constantly in a minority of one on the Board of a dynamic and growing organization. When recession hit, he was the first to be made redundant, even though the company later retrenched to the position that he had been advocating. Several hundred people unnecessarily lost their jobs.

For Keith, the lesson learned was that being right doesn't count for anything in the overall scheme of things. He has been made redundant twice more since that first time and now sees his future in short-term, highly paid, interim management contracts.

What we know from our research for this book is that many long-term unemployed people believe that their skills, experience and knowledge are not valued in their search for employment:

> I've been unemployed for two years. I'm a British Telecom, Government PBX-trained telephonist and receptionist. I have experience on all up-to-date computerized and screen-based switchboards. I am reliable, never late for work, smartly dressed, well-spoken, and can work on my own initiative, work well in a team of all ages and communicate with people of all levels. I cope under pressure, am willing to help in other fields, keep calm with irate people, have an excellent personality and am excellent at my work. Still, I cannot get a job. I am registered with every employment agency in London. My newspaper bill is over £13 per week, and I have to spend at least £30 per week on travel to try to find work, plus shoe leather as I'm tramping the streets looking for work. I'm told I come over well at interviews. I wear a suit and all my clothes match, including my handbag and shoes, but still no luck.
>
> I now seriously believe that, because I am a mature lady of 46, companies will not employ people of my age because I'm not a dolly bird any more.

There is a deep feeling of hopelessness in many of the letters we have read from people who are convinced they are doing more than their level best to find work, but consistently fail to do so:

> Why don't employers want competent, honest, experienced people? I used to work on the research technical staff of a major manufacturer. Some years after I started with the company, I took an aptitude test for their computer division and found out later that I had passed with one

of the best marks ever. But, my transfer was disallowed because I was told I did not have the right attitude to the company. After that, with great reluctance, I was allowed to start a part-time degree course in physics. The Manager told me, 'If you get this degree, which I don't for one moment think you will, I won't make you senior staff because you are the wrong sort of person.' Needless to say, I left and they gave me six months' salary. I then went into science teaching, but this was a disaster. Most teacher trainees are much younger and as a mature student aged over 40 with real industrial scientific experience, I was an embarrassment. I found actual teaching in a school no better – where I was accused of expecting too much of the children. I am now unemployed and looking for a scientific/technical/engineering job where I know I have a lot to offer.

What is so sad and worrying about this man's letter is that the bitterness and anger he so obviously feels may well have contributed both to his experiences in his first job, where, somehow, he had managed to antagonize the people who might have encouraged and promoted him, as well as his failure as a student teacher. I can't help feeling that he may have been an angry, bitter man even *before* he became an employee and that this trait of his personality will hinder him for ever in his search for employment, unless he can come to terms with himself and, perhaps, seek help to approach life and relationships more positively.

Trading down market

It's natural to think that if you can't find work in the area in which you are best qualified, then it makes sense to pursue something less skilful. Whether you're a senior executive trading down into junior management or a craftsperson seeking unskilled production line work, just think how this looks to a prospective employer. Did you lose your last job because you'd been overpromoted? Are you trying to get a foot in the door before making a 'power play'? Are you just biding your time until the 'right' opportunity comes along?

> I feel that once you have been self-employed, particularly if you have had your own company, you are at a great disadvantage when it comes to getting employment. I am a man of 49. At one time, I had a very successful catering business. During the 16 years I had the business, I interviewed literally hundreds of job applicants. However, when the recession caused my business to collapse, I hit the job market thinking I had lots to offer. I have been searching for an executive position for nearly two years, without luck. I believe my

interview techniques are good and I always analyse the interview afterwards. As time goes on I am convinced that I do not get a job for the following reasons. First, the interviewer is afraid I know more than he does and his job might be in danger. Second, that I might want to boss people around and be unable to take orders, and, finally, that I am far too overqualified, having been a director of my own company, for them to take me on.

Incidentally, I never cease to be amazed at the shoddy way interviews are carried out. Either the interviewer hasn't got a clue how to interview or they make you feel as if they're just going through the motions and haven't the slightest intention of employing you. I often think it's just an opportunity for them to talk at someone without having to listen! Needless to say I am disillusioned – and still out of work.

For anyone who *does* find work at a lower level, it should only ever be on the understanding that it is for a definite trial period. It's quite understandable that a new employer should ask you to prove your abilities, but quite unreasonable to expect you to undertake a test that is without either finite objectives or a clear ending. If there is no prospect of the position translating into permanent employment, that should be made clear at the start, and you should consider whether or not an alternative form of employment might be more appropriate. Discussing this issue sometimes has other advantages, particularly in terms of focusing both parties' attention on the role to be undertaken.

Self-employment

The Department of Employment takes a dim view of employers who attempt to avoid National Insurance contributions by hiring staff on a self-employed basis. Although the rules are quite strict, it is possible to trade as a self-employed contractor or consultant, with financial advantages to both company and worker.

One way of giving yourself that edge is to do the same job for a cheaper rate than your prospective competitors. Note, too, that after adding employer's costs, such as National Insurance payments, pension contributions and paid holidays, the actual cost of an employee to a company is about 25 per cent more than their basic salary package. If you add a car, then the employee costs nearly 40 per cent on top of their basic salary.

If you're considering self-employment read the rules carefully. Read *Self-Employed?*, a booklet published by the Benefits Agency, leaflet FB30. See if you qualify. Naturally, there are advantages and disadvantages to being self-employed, but the principal advantage is that you may be able to avoid simply becoming another figure in the unemployment statistics.

Setting up a limited company

There are many people who set themselves up as limited companies in order to circumvent the self-employment regulations, but it must be remembered that if you're a company you must comply with company law.

Setting up a company is surprisingly quick and cheap. You can buy one 'off the shelf' from company formation agents who advertise in national newspapers' business sections, for around £100 to £150. However, it is wise not to do so before you've taken advice from both an accountant and a solicitor. There can be quite substantial costs in meeting your legal obligations.

Setting up a small company

There are a number of books dealing with this subject and we cannot go into it in much detail here, but, if this is an option you are considering, it is *essential* that the decision is one that is taken with the full cooperation and endorsement of your partner and, where appropriate, the rest of your family.

Business start-up loans

A warning: most loans and grants have to be repaid one way or another and collateral will be required. If you borrow money from the bank to start a business and use your home as a collateral, you stand to lose the roof over your head if the business fails.

Once again, you need to know yourself. If you've never been a risktaker while working for somebody else, you're unlikely to make that change too readily. Such factors must be remembered at all times, but it can, and has, been done successfully!

Job creation schemes

Training and Enterprise Councils (TECs) are now the principal means by which Government money is channelled into job creation schemes. The quality of help and assistance offered by TECs is variable. For example, to my knowledge, the board of one TEC decided to target its money in three specific areas – construction, farming and tourism. Unfortunately, it took that decision in 1990, after the start of the worst recession in the construction industry in living memory, after the Lockerbie bomb had temporarily all but wiped out international air travel, and at a time when the then EEC was paying out millions annually in 'set aside' land.

Working from home

If you're setting up a small business, becoming a freelance consultant or even taking up a job that is specially designed so that you can work from home, clearly it's essential that you plan and prepare the actual part of your home that will be given over for the 'office' or place of work. Using the dining-room table or, worse still, the kitchen table without first having a serious family discussion about it is bound to lead to resentment and irritation. Using the bedroom, or a corner of it, as an office needs careful management, too.

Planning and making clear, objective assessments of your experience in life and work so far, and working, with your partner's help, advice and perhaps insight, to promote these towards the areas of possible future employment which seem most likely to be successful will, in itself, be an experience which should strengthen your relationship. You'll be *doing* something positive.

6
What can I do to help?

To re-emphasize a point we made earlier, the key to survival after a redundancy in the family is *teamwork*.

If a good relationship can be compared to a successful business partnership, then the bad times and the disasters that crop up must be shared just as the good times can be. And management decisions should be shared, too – on a 'two heads are better than one' basis.

For some men, it seems strange to discuss their working or 'business' life with their partner. They've been used to keeping that part of their daily life in a separate compartment to that of the home and family. Many women are happy with this and are content to have a 'Good day at the office, dear?' level of involvement. But, when redundancy strikes, there is no option *but* to become involved on a much deeper level and on an equal basis – if only because both partners are directly affected by the results of the loss of income, change of circumstances and, sometimes, loss of status in the local or wider world they inhabit.

The need to help

Most partners feel as angry, hurt and shocked as the one who's lost the job, and there's an instinctive urge to want to help, to be as supportive and encouraging as possible. A prime example is Sylvia's letter, which asked for, 'advice on what problems are likely to arise and how I can help him to deal with them'.

Of course, there's an element of self-interest in this reaction because the partner is also anxious about what the future may hold for *them* and how it will affect their own life. There's often also a sense of powerlessness. They're feeling some of the same emotions and fears, but have much less control in terms of doing something about changing the situation, of finding new work. Their life is bound to be changed too, and they have no option but to make changes and adaptations, which might not be what they wanted.

Even for couples who really work as a team, there are likely to be problems and pitfalls. As the Relate counsellors at Northampton reported:

> Redundant people become very narrow in outlook. All they can think of is that they've lost their job and have much less money and the

future is bleak. They often feel resentful that they're put into a position of having to listen to what other people are saying and telling them.

Other people who take on the role of 'adviser' – especially people close to them who want to help – can become an irritation rather than be seen as a positive benefit.

Partners need to tread carefully to avoid setting up a 'block' from the other side of the team. As Nicky said:

> Mike would have sat silent for ever. He'd always have an excuse for not talking about the problem, like 'not in front of the children'.

So, the tactics have to be a careful estimation of how far you can push without overstepping the line between 'bossing' and 'helping'.

Simple ways to help

There are lots of fairly obvious ways of helping with the new project of looking for a new job. First, making a space at home for an office area where the work can be done with as little disruption and interruption as possible. The kitchen table is not the best location to choose, therefore! If there's a spare room, you're lucky, but most of us have to find a corner of the dining room or, often, a bedroom.

If the family possesses a word processor, it will make a huge difference, but, if not, a good electric typewriter will suffice, as long as the typist is very accurate or there's an effective correction device! If not, a first consideration might be whether or not to buy a basic personal computer with a word processing system or a good second-hand word processor.

Helping to draw up a list of contacts who might know of another opening – telephone contacts and those to be done by letter – can be very useful, as can drafting the letters to go to these contacts. Checking and rechecking the spelling is vital and a second pair of eyes can make all the difference. Invest in a good dictionary if there isn't one in the house.

Drawing up a list of companies or organizations that might be good prospects for speculative letters and compiling the list of names of people, spelt correctly, to whom the letters will be addressed is another excellent way of helping.

Drafting a new CV and getting books from the library on how to do this is useful (see also Chapter 7). While there, find books about looking for new work from among the many on the library shelves (see also Further reading section at the end of this book).

Get involved in deciding on which newspapers, local and national as well as the specialist trade or professional publications, to get by seeing which carry advertisements for the sorts of jobs that might be suitable. These will need to be ordered from the newsagent and are a necessary expense.

Being encouraging – but avoiding nagging (a difficult line to draw!) – is helpful. Also, agree that the project of finding a job will be worked at between specific hours in the day. So, if you've decided that the jobseeker will work between 9 and 5 pm, don't ask them to go to the supermarket with you in the middle of the morning – unless you decide that the time will be made up later and you can be sure that this won't be forgotten!

Obviously, as, in a sense, your partner is now working for themselves, they can fit their hours of work in to suit themselves or the family's plans. But, the point is that no one should forget that their job, for the time being, is to get a new job.

Talking and planning

Planning some sort of timetable and for the future is a way of making things seem less unstructured and uncertain. Some outplacement counsellors recommend that a six-month contingency plan should be drawn up, so that both partners and the rest of the family, too, if appropriate, have an idea of what to expect.

Work out the finances for that period and budget accordingly. If the average length of time it takes to find new work is reducing at the moment, the period out of work may not be as long as six months. It may, of course, take longer for the right job – or, indeed, any job – to come up, in which case you can extend the plan by another three months, six months or whatever is right at that time. Planning in this way and having a programme to work to tends to take the uncertainty out of the situation, and it is uncertainty about the future that is so difficult for anyone to live with.

When Chris was made redundant from his job in sales, for the second time, when the recession was at its deepest, he and his wife Helen, who's a speech therapist, decided to try to keep things as normal as possible for the next six months and live on her salary. If after that time he still hadn't found a job, they planned to consider other options, such as swapping roles on a permanent basis, studying for further qualifications for Chris or moving to a smaller house.

As we saw earlier, one of Wendy's first thoughts was that she and Colin could swap jobs. Her job for the last six years has been running their home as a bed and breakfast. Before that she was teaching in adult education in the fashion and textile industry.

We'd occasionally talked about swapping jobs before and I thought that was instantly the answer, because of our peculiar circumstances here. I thought it was a job he could eventually do. We'd talked about that and I would go out and look for a job, but it was unrealistic because I've been out of the job market for six years, so I'd have to retrain.

Swapping roles

For some couples, the idea of exchanging roles in the household and family seems exciting and challenging. For some dads, becoming a 'house husband' seems like a way of becoming involved in their children's lives in a way that would be impossible while working a full week. For some, it can even be seen as an honourable escape from having to go out and sell themselves in the hard commercial world again, having been turned out by one employer.

However, if a complete role reversal – changing to become a full-time, house-based parent while the partner who formerly did this returns to full-time employment – is to work well, both of you have to be rather special, very adaptable and very unselfish. Quite often I've heard of fathers who stay at home with the children being quite happy organizing the ferrying of the children about to nursery, playground or school and back, but finding it impossible to also fit in the cleaning, washing and shopping!

Penny and Dave

Friends of mine, Penny and Dave, both leapt at the opportunity of changing jobs when he opted to take redundancy from the family firm he'd worked in for over 20 years when it was scaling down.

The plan, theoretically, was for Dave to be at home for their two children, take them to school and collect them and, in between, he would have time to press on with the renovation of the large Victorian house they'd not long moved into.

Penny found it harder than she'd expected to find full-time work as a secretary after nearly ten years of part-time and voluntary work, but, after a few months, she found a job at the local Council Offices, which meant the travel costs were low.

The change in roles led, over time, to changes in their personalities and then in their relationship. Dave realized he'd gone into his former job straight from school without thinking it through carefully enough. Now, he found he wanted to do much more with his life and he used the opportunity of not having to go out every day to work to explore his personal potential and his ambitions for the future. He became involved with political movements, alternative therapies and the Men's Movement and and a whole new world opened up for him.

Although he said he wanted Penny to be involved with all this, she found it difficult, mostly because she did not share his political views and opinions. She found it irritating that, not only was she still doing the household chores, which Dave didn't seem to notice needed doing, but the house she'd wanted to do so much with was still largely in the same state as it was when they moved in!

She, too, was changing. Going back to work full time, after a shaky start, gave back some of the confidence in herself and her abilities that she'd felt she'd lost while being at home with the children. Then, after nine months in her first job, she saw an advertisement for the sort of job she'd always dreamed of. Penny applied for it, and was offered it, and her life took off.

Changing roles, for Penny and Dave, had allowed them to get through a difficult change in the financial and family situation, but for them, as it happened, it also led to them rethinking themselves and their relationship with each other. Five years after the role swap, Penny left Dave to live alone on the other side of the city. Their children stayed with their father, partly because they were at a crucial stage in their education and also because, by that time, they were used to Dad being in charge at home.

Changes in life can be opportunities. Sometimes they can be opportunities for changes that we may not have expected or wished for.

Eight months after Colin's redundancy, by the time he'd realized the new job was not a success, Wendy was thinking again about swapping jobs. Perhaps I telephoned on a bad day or at a bad time, but there was a definite note of irritation in Wendy's voice as she reported on the current situation six months after Colin began the new job:

Colin absolutely hates it! He just sticks it out for the money, and even that's unreliable. Last month's money was a month late being paid.

He isn't doing anything about finding any other job. He halfheartedly looks when I find him something advertised, but always says he wouldn't be suitable for it.

I've been thinking about finding another job myself. In fact, just today I saw a job advertised locally which I'd be ideal for. It's just down the road and it has school holidays.

I've been trying to find out how to brush up my teaching qualifications, but, when I enquire, people ask me why I want more? You have to be very persistent to find out about courses and what's available. Anyway, there are no courses round here.

> It annoys me when I think of all the money spent on my training and now I can't use it. I feel I'm a willing horse that's being shoved away from the water.

She and Colin had been talking again about him taking over the running of the B&B:

> But I don't think he'll do my job properly. And I'm not sure if Colin doing the B&B is the right thing.

Dangers and disputes

There are dangers involved in changing roles in a relationship. When we meet and decide to commit ourselves to someone, we bring with us to the partnership our own beliefs and thinking about the role each should play within it. They're beliefs based in our childhood, upbringing and from the family we knew as we grew up. They're beliefs and – more dangerously – assumptions about male and female roles generally in a relationship. Changes to any of these feel frightening, threatening, and how we react depends on our views and our previous experiences of life and relationships, and the way we feel about ourselves, our personal security.

When I spoke to her that day, I think Wendy was not only saying how she thought *Colin* felt about doing her job as the manager of the B&B business, but also expressing her own feelings about him taking over *her* role. Quite plainly, she didn't like the idea one bit! But, when she said she thought that running the B&B business wouldn't be a worthwhile, useful or challenging enough job for Colin, what I think she was saying was that, in her estimation, it wasn't a 'manly' enough job for him.

Wendy is a very perceptive, intelligent person, but, somewhere in her belief system, there's something that informs her that a man 'puts on a suit and tie' and goes out to work. That a 'proper man' – or, perhaps, a man she would prefer not to be married to – doesn't put on a pinny and set to work cleaning the skirting boards! The fact that owning and running a bed and breakfast business is not only a very useful service, but inevitably brings the manager into daily contact with a wide range of people, seemed to have been forgotten.

The reality is that women, generally, even in this day and age, find it difficult to give up our their usual role – or the way they see their role in the relationship and in the family – to men. This seems to be no different from the reluctance men have, for several generations, shown regarding giving up what have traditionally been seen as male roles and hitherto male-dominated spheres of work and business. An explanation for all this is the natural fear, on both sides, of being taken over, swallowed up and absorbed by the other side.

In the world of big business, men are slowly becoming used to women in the boardroom. Some are adjusting to having a woman as a boss. Even the macho world of football has accepted a woman manager of a team – not just in a fictional TV show, but in reality. In some areas, however, notably the armed forces and especially the Royal Navy, workers are being torn apart by disputes over equality between the sexes – particularly regarding women serving at sea. The BBC TV series *HMS Brilliant*, a fly-on-the-wall view of life on one naval ship and the people who live in such closely confined conditions within it for months at a time, included an episode about women at sea. It gave a particularly fascinating view of the difficulties both sexes find in working alongside each other on, theoretically, equal terms.

Overturning long-held attitudes about male and female roles takes many generations, so mistakes are bound to be made and there will be casualties along the way. It isn't at all surprising, therefore, that when the man in the family loses his accepted role as the major wage earner and takes over the woman's accepted role in the household, even if it is for only a short time, there are arguments about the right way to vacuum the stairs or hang out the washing!

Think it through

So, if you and your partner are considering exchanging roles, it's important to be aware of your inbuilt attitudes to your roles and to be able to discuss the possibility in a rational and reasonable way.

If you, as the partner who has not suffered redundancy, have a job that might help you survive financially for the time being while adjustments are being made or while a new job for your partner is being found, then obviously it would be silly *not* to consider swapping roles.

As a member of a team, you have to be prepared to pull your weight – or even be ready to do *more* than your fair share, on occasions – in the interests of the team as a whole.

Balance

True teamwork is all about balance. It's about two people, who are themselves individuals, finding a mutually beneficial way of balancing and complementing each other in order to provide a comfortable and enjoyable life together. Any upset to this balance is going to cause problems and stress for the couple and for the relationship. Susie Orbach, in *Women, Men and Marriage* (Sheldon Press, 1995) wrote:

WHAT CAN I DO TO HELP?

We bring to marriage a desire to express and receive love, to exchange companionship, erotic intimacy, our needs for attachment, and to fulfil a wish to have our individuality supported and extended from the base of a stable and secure relationship.

Almost everything we desire from marriage, including the hearts-and-flowers imagery which pervades our notions of romance, expresses in their deepest conceptions, differences between men and women in the understanding of these desires.

Relationships are hard work, and anyone going into one does so at their own risk!

It's inevitable, therefore, that when a major problem, like redundancy and unemployment, hits there will need to be major changes and major efforts on the part of both partners to survive and control the situation. So, if a decision is taken to go ahead with a role swap or some other change, then both partners need to be in agreement about this. Unfortunately, such decisions are likely to be made of necessity rather than choice because of the situation, but, if the change is seen as being a feasible solution to an otherwise insoluble problem, then it's more likely to be workable. If one partner feels forced into something they don't really want to do, however, the risk that resentment will build up to become destructive is great.

'Why should I?'

If the partner who didn't lose their job starts saying, or thinking without saying, things like, 'Why should I . . .

- have to put up with you round my feet all day
- have to scrimp and save
- have to go without a holiday
- have to disrupt the children's lives
- have to go back to work'

especially if they don't feel able to say these things to their already depressed partner, that's when trouble can start! It's OK to feel and be angry about what's happened. In fact, it's probably healthier to do this than to keep it suppressed. But, for the sake of the relationship, it's obviously better not to get angry with each other too often and too destructively.

'I went away and got angry by myself or talked to my friends', one wife confided. She felt that, for her husband's sake, she had to be the one who put on the brave front and tried to remain calm and optimistic.

If, on the other hand, one partner does say these things out loud, then some kind of trouble was probably already there in the relationship and it may need to be addressed in a different way, ideally with counselling for the couple and the relationship.

Showing up the cracks

Redundancy and unemployment show up the cracks in a relationship very quickly. 'You have to be very together to survive it together', said my sister-in-law, who has survived it twice. Many couples have found that, in the end, the efforts they've made together to deal with the problems – joining forces against a common 'enemy' – have brought them much closer together than they'd been for years. Others are not so lucky.

If you already knew cracks were there, but you'd ignored them or papered over them, then, at such a time, it will be right to face up to the problems and tackle them. The Relate counsellors at Northampton have seen many couples who've reached deadlock. They're trapped in that terrible spiral of either being able to talk but going round and round in circles getting nowhere or of being unable to talk about the problems at all. These couples have taken the often last-resort decision to make an appointment with Relate.

For some, there is an awareness that the loss of one partner's job and livelihood has caused the cracks in the relationship to open up to a point where they need to build a bridge across them, and they want Relate to help them construct the bridge.

For others, the problem is seen as being one partner's depression, anger, violence or impotence and it isn't until later on, as the sessions with the counsellor progress, that the issue of the redundancy and subsequent unemployment is raised.

So, if you're constantly arguing over what you should do about the situation or blaming each other or refusing to talk about it or one of you is becoming obviously and seriously depressed, then you need to ask for help. The next chapter looks at how to find help – for your relationship and for the family before it falls apart.

7
Getting help and helping yourself

There *is* help around – the trick is knowing what help there is, what it's for and how to get it.

There are Government-sponsored help and information agencies, like the Employment Service, the Benefits Agency, and Jobclubs.

This book isn't specifically about finding a new job – there are a lot of books to help you or your partner do that, some we've found to be good are listed at the end of this book. Finding these, at the library or a bookshop, is something you can do together, though, and some couples find that it is helpful if they both read a book and then pool the information they've found within it. Two people pick up quite different things from the same chapter!

Letting people know

What is essential is that you both understand the importance of letting people know that you are out of work and looking for a new job. Information and advice about this is given in any book about redundancy and unemployment, but it bears repeating. Major problems and serious debt can be avoided if individuals and organizations like banks, building societies, your landlord, the gas, electricity and water and telephone companies and the local authority are informed of your new circumstances sooner rather than later. All the lending agencies and utility companies have customer service departments whose staff are specially trained to help people cope with sudden loss of income caused by various situations, including job loss. Look on the back of your gas bill, for instance, for information about where to get help and advice and telephone, or write to the address given.

All of these companies and organizations say that they would far rather help a borrower or customer adjust their monthly or quarterly payments straight away than have to spend time sorting out serious debt later on, let alone having, for instance, to repossess a home and sell it off. So, even if it takes some courage and you feel embarrassed about it, make a list of the people you need to inform and tick them off one by one.

Sean, a Senior Debt Counselling Officer in Northampton and also a Relate Counsellor, told me that clients who come to him with debt problems generally fall into two categories:

Some people will go for help even before they're made redundant. They know there's a chance of it and they're planning ahead. They're up front – they can anticipate there will be losses and want to get in there before it happens and minimize it. They're budgeting sensibly in their approach to money and can be helped and organized quite simply.

Others will come through the door when something terrible has just happened. I call it the 'ostrich syndrome'. They just completely ignore everything that's happened – all the signs that could be warning them – and they'll walk in for help, with a repossession notice clutched in their hand. For instance, yesterday I had someone walk in with an eviction notice – it's not uncommon. Not only an eviction notice for next week, but a court hearing in two days' time and today they're up for committal for non-payment of Council Tax, and also they've got a TV licence fine outstanding, with a warrant out for their arrest on it, and their water's been disconnected. They've ignored it all until yesterday. But, in fact, this couple did come and see me two months ago and I organized it all for them and gave them advice and they haven't done a sausage, not one thing! And he just sat there with his eyes brimming, hardly saying anything.

One of Sean's Relate colleagues chipped in with a comparison between this couple and a couple who come for relationship counselling who simply cannot take the steps that need to be taken and have to be urged along the way:

It's one of the functions that isn't there – the ability to do anything.

It's worth highlighting that no matter how much help there is out there, if people are not willing to actually take it, nobody's going to be able to help them and they're going to become one of those appalling statistics.

Once again, it becomes clear that the way you handle this situation will depend on the sort of person and family you are, and the sort of experiences you've already been through in life. If you're already fairly competent at handling money and staying within a budget, you won't have too much difficulty in adjusting and adapting to the new situation – once you've got over the initial shock of it all. *No one* finds it easy to think clearly when they're in a state of severe shock. If, on the other hand, you feel swamped and overwhelmed by worry about how to sort out the financial problems, *please* seek advice and help and be ready to act on it (see under the heading Advisory services later in this chapter).

Another thing on which all the advisers and counsellors I talked to were agreed was the importance of telling anyone and everyone who might be helpful that you're looking for a new job. It's natural, at first, for many people to feel embarrassed about admitting they've been 'let go' or that their partner has been made redundant. But, as redundancy is now so common in British society, there should be no need for embarrassment or shame. The in word for spreading the news is 'networking'.

Networking

Most of us have a 'network' of family, extended family, friends, neighbours, people we've kept in touch with over time and people we've met through work, sport or hobbies at various stages in our lives. We don't even think about this network most of the time because these people are just part of our lives. But, in times of trouble, we look to our friends and people who love and like us for support and help. That's what friends are for.

The point of letting these people – or at least a selected group of them – know that you're out of work is that they might know someone who knows someone who might have just the job for you!

Research – mostly by marketing organizations concerned with what became known as pyramid selling – indicates that, on average, each person knows at least 50 other people. Each of these people knows another 50, and so on and so on. Another claim is that it should be possible to get through to speak to anyone you want or need to by making five telephone calls – if only you know which one to start with! Also, of course, if you have the right computer system and are on the Internet, you can communicate with anyone in the world – as long as they are also connected to the system.

But to get back to the reality of your situation. The point of networking is to give yourself the best possible chance of getting started again and back into the world of work – if, of course, that's where you decide you want to be. Even if you decide *not* to go back into paid employment, you'll need to find out how to do what you want to do with the rest of your life. So, use your network.

A man known to Michael Witcher, who was made redundant when his factory closed down, got chatting over the garden fence to his next-door neighbour. This man was able to tell him that he'd seen a notice in his factory advertising recruitment only that week. He went along the following Monday, and got a job!

There's no doubt that luck plays a great role in life! There's also no doubt that getting a job today, at whatever level, is often about who you know. There's a reluctance, particularly for small companies and organizations, to have to go through all the hassle and expense of advertising a vacancy, going through the avalanche of replies and then a series of interviews. People now tend to think about whether they know anyone who might want the job or ask colleagues or friends if they know anyone. This is another reason for thinking about your contacts and networking, especially if there's a specific grapevine in your particular field of work or interest.

Advisory services

Remember the national advisory services, too. We mentioned the statutory employment and social services agencies at the beginning of this chapter, and the Citizens Advice Bureau is an excellent resource. There are 720 main offices dotted all over the country, plus other smaller offices opening once or twice a week in village halls, health centres and hospitals, making a total of around 1,500 Citizens Advice Bureau outlets. All these provide a professional service for anyone about almost anything.

Advising individuals and couples on budgeting and debt, especially as a result of redundancy, now makes up the majority of the Bureau's work, and the staff are well-equipped to help. Many Bureaux have special debt counselling units, which have been set up to cope with the increasing number of enquiries it receives on this subject.

Requests for help with employment and unemployment, redundancy payments, pension arrangements and advice about dismissal have doubled in the last decade. Also, the subject of housing, including rent arrears, mortgage arrears and the threat of homelessness, is the fourth commonest area people ask for help with.

The national information system is available to all centres, so the help a Bureau is able to offer is as up to date as it is possible to be. Look in your local telephone directory or under the heading Counselling and advice in the *Yellow Pages* to find the address of your nearest Citizens Advice Bureau. Some centres now operate an appointment system and others offer telephone advice in certain circumstances.

Going to your local Citizens Advice Bureau would be our first recommendation for getting help to sort out practical problems as a result of redundancy. The staff there will be able to advise you about other areas of worry, too, such as how to keep up regular payments and avoid getting into debt, and let you know if there are any benefits you might be entitled to.

A note about benefits

This is a complicated area – with rules that change all the time – so it's worth checking to see if you qualify for help. One woman remembers that her husband was reluctant to ask for State help:

He wasn't going to sign on and claim benefit at first, but I persuaded him to go along. 'Think of all the money you've paid in National Insurance all your working life', I said.

Paid-for help and advice

There are various services you can call on to help you cope with redundancy and its effects – in terms of surviving as a couple and a family as well as searching for new work.

Outplacement counselling

This is a relatively new growth area in counselling. Michael Witcher, of Witcher-Stronge Selection, explains that the term is jargon for 'between job career counselling'. He says that most people should now expect, in a working lifespan, to have several periods 'between jobs', and that planning for these spaces in life should be a normal, accepted part of our thinking and expectations.

Outplacement counselling, more and more, is being provided by companies and industries for their departing employees as part of a redundancy package. For some managers and executives, there will be individual sessions and sometimes their partners will be invited to take part. For others, there will be group sessions and seminars that take people through a similar programme of information and advice to help them move on towards the next period of work. Individuals can then, if they wish, take up topics of particular interest at a separate meeting with the consultants.

If you have a chance to receive outplacement counselling, take it! If a human resources consultancy has been contracted to work with your whole factory or company – or a whole department if your organization is downsizing – it will have wide local and national resources to call upon, and you should take advantage of these.

CVs and CV-writing services

One crucial item for anyone wanting to find new work is an up-to-date curriculum vitae, or, as it is more commonly called, a CV. Helping you prepare one is an important part of the services offered by outplacement counsellors, but you can employ someone to write yours for you. There are frequently advertisements in local and national newspapers from companies that offer this service. If you decide to have a CV written, you still need to provide the firm with information about yourself, so, unless you merely use a CV-writing agency to provide you with professionally presented documents, the advice from the human resources and recruitment professionals is to do it yourself!

Writing your CV

As Clare Stronge says, if you asked 20 human resource managers or recruitment consultants what the best, most successful CV should look like, you'd get 20 different answers! However, what they would all agree is that a good CV should be typed or word-processed on good-quality A4-size paper and, preferably, be only two pages long.

If you're not using the services of a consultancy, I suggest you look in one or more of the many books about successful jobseeking for examples and guidelines on how to put together a CV. Find the most up-to-date, too, because there are fashions in CVs, just as there are fashions in everything else in life, and you don't want to look old-fashioned! (See also the Further reading section at the end of this book.)

The purpose of your CV is to act as your prospectus, to tell the employer what you can do, what you've done so far and the skills you would bring to a particular position.

An example of the sort of help outplacement counsellors can give in this area – which you might be able to think about for yourself or, better still, work at as a team project – is the exercise called 'competency profiling'. As Michael Witcher said:

> If someone comes to me and says, 'I've been working there for 20 years, I don't know how to do anything else', I sit them down and go through everything they've ever done since the day they were born. It's called 'threads analysis'. It's to pick out anything they've done or been involved in which has provided them with skills and resources that can equip them for employment or for earning money.

So, if you were a prefect at school or in the netball team, especially if you were a captain, that experience can go on your skills list as 'team leading'. If you've been at home, running the household and coping with two or three small children, you've most certainly acquired 'time management and organizational skills'.

Try to think of everything – and then some more – put it all down on paper and then prune it or edit it down so you end up with a concise, informative and effective document, to 'sell' you and what you have to offer.

Someone else who knows you well can be a great help in constructing and devising your prospectus. Your partner's input can be useful, as can those from your network of supporters.

Jobclubs

These can be a very useful and helpful resource for unemployed people searching for work. If you haven't got the facilities at home, your local Jobclub provides a desk, telephone, typewriter, photocopier, stationery and stamps, as well as directories and newspapers. It is also a 'place to go' and offers companionship with people in the same boat. There's also advice and guidance on job-seeking techniques. You need to have been unemployed for six months or more and be looking for a job rather than for further training, and you have to be prepared to go there at least four times a week, usually for half a day and commit yourself to following up ten job leads every day.

There are also Supportive Jobclubs for people with disabilities and specialized groups, such as ex-offenders, ex-service people and executives.

Setting up a Jobclub

Most Jobclubs are set up and run by voluntary groups, such as churches or ethnic community groups or private individuals. So, anyone can make a proposal and apply to the Regional Employment Service for funding to start a Jobclub, with its advice and support. Thus, if you don't have a Jobclub near you, perhaps you or a couple or group of people can make an opportunity for and also benefit others.

Getting help for yourself

You may feel that you, your partner and the family will manage to get through this trauma on your own or with the help of your family and friends. Many people can and do, but some individuals and couples feel that they could use and benefit from some outside, objective help with what is going on in their heads or what is happening in their relationship.

Counselling

This is much to be recommended if, at any time, you feel you're going round and round in circles with each other and with your relationship and getting nowhere or that things are getting you down.

Often the reaction to this suggestion is a rather bored, 'Oh no, not counselling again', or the question, 'Why does everyone have to be offered counselling all the time for every little thing?'

The problem is that the word counselling is used for everything from post-traumatic stress counselling after major disasters, such as the sinking of the ferry at Zeebrugge, to relationship or marital counselling and everything in between, such as rape crisis counselling and bereavement counselling.

People also ask what happened when people suffered these disasters in previous generations? Sometimes the question is asked with a kind of 'We didn't make a fuss, we just got on with it' attitude. It's almost as if it's seen as a weakness to seek counselling support. Of course this is one of the reasons many people, especially men, find it difficult to accept that counselling can be helpful, even necessary.

In the not too distant past, of course, the world was rather smaller and communities were often closer than they tend to be now. Families, too, were often larger and more close-knit and supportive than many can be today. So, perhaps it was easier to find someone to turn to, to talk it out with and unburden yourself to. Perhaps, though, we look on the past as a golden age and problems just got buried and festered away.

Counselling may seem like a new phenomenon, but the Marriage Guidance Council (which was renamed Relate in 1988) was founded in 1938, and Samaritans was begun by Reverend Chad Varah in 1953, so the need for help has certainly been around for some time. Perhaps it's because communication is now so much more extensive that we know more about it.

Counselling took off in the 1980s, but the British Association for Counselling – a body devoted to promoting and regulating counselling standards – was set up in January 1978.

Make counselling work for you

When counselling is suggested, it's usually to help with a relationship that has reached crisis point. 'But surely we can sort it out between ourselves?', one or both partners may say. The difficulty is that, when emotions are strained, a 'quiet talk' quickly becomes an acrimonious dispute, a 'sensible chat' ends with one in tears and the other rushing from the room slamming the door.

Counselling isn't right for everyone or the answer to every problem but talking in the presence of an impartial person can make a big difference. It works best when you have some idea of what to expect and are prepared to put a lot of effort into it.

'We've been to marriage guidance and it didn't work', some say – they've 'tried counselling' and come away confused, disappointed and disillusioned. Others say, 'It took me weeks to get him to Relate, but, after the first session, he wouldn't go again'. Indeed, men rarely take the initiative to seek counselling. Most find it very difficult to talk about feelings, especially to a stranger, and it seems very threatening. They're more likely to agree to go as a last-ditch attempt to save the relationship or if their partner's been talking to a counsellor first, to make sure their side of the story is told. If they feel counselling isn't solving the problem instantly or if they've felt criticized, they won't go back.

What counselling is and isn't

The counsellor usually starts by asking why you're there. You tell the story and, by interrupting you occasionally and asking questions, checks what you mean and what you think or feel.

Often, it's the explanations you give that throw new light on a problem you thought you'd seen from every angle. If you've been getting nowhere, this can be a huge relief – or it can be quite scary.

There are no magic wands to solve your problem or make it go away. A counsellor can't do it for you.

Why bother to go to see a counsellor, then – wouldn't a heart-to-heart with your mother, another relative or a close friend be as good?

They can listen, but they'll be involved with you and your life and have their own feelings about it, which will colour their opinions. A counsellor, however, knows nothing about you, except what you tell them. Counsellors are trained to separate their own feelings from whatever you talk about and concentrate exclusively on you. And, after a series of sessions with a counsellor, you need never see them again, so you can be completely frank and open.

Don't make the mistake of thinking that counselling is an easy option. Seeing yourself or your relationship in a new light can be painful. Hearing your partner say, 'You give all your love to the kids and I feel left out', could shake you rigid if he's never said it at home. But the counsellor's there to help you both face up to what each of you say, see if there is a valid point in such statements and work out how to deal with it.

Is it for you?

Use counselling only if you're prepared to make changes in yourself, your behaviour or your relationship. Then, the outcome will be worth the effort you put into it – whatever that outcome may be.

Depression

Depression can take many forms and is an all too common result of redundancy and unemployment. It is essential that you and your family be aware of the signals pointing to serious depression and the dangers of ignoring them. The trouble is, when you're close to a person and living with them day to day, it's easy to get used to little, gradual changes in someone's personality, attitude or habits and not take any notice of them.

If you or your partner:

- becomes more tired than usual
- goes to bed earlier, but either doesn't sleep or wakes up earlier in the morning
- can't be bothered with much or anything
- loses interest in something they've always enjoyed or loses interest in everything
- doesn't bother to get up or get dressed in the morning

- can't be bothered to wash, shampoo their hair or shave
- becomes irritable and short-tempered
- goes off sex

they could be suffering symptoms of depression. This is not the ordinary kind of 'feeling a bit low' depression. Someone who's lost their job and is out of work would be pretty unusual if they didn't go through a period of feeling miserable afterwards! In fact, stress counsellors and people working with the unemployed say that it is important to go through a 'mourning' or grieving stage as a way of drawing one period of time, and work, to a close before beginning the next one. Rather, this is the sort of depression that is overwhelming, all-absorbing and seems impossible to escape from.

Depression is a serious illness needing medical and therapeutic treatment, so it's important not to ignore the possibility that depression can strike down someone who has suffered a traumatic shock and blow to their self-esteem and self-confidence. Therefore, if you're worried that you or your partner might even be near enough to the edge of despair to feel suicidal, then don't waste time wondering. Get them to a telephone to talk to the Samaritans or talk to the Samaritans yourself about your fears. You can contact the Samaritans all over the UK using just one telephone number: 0345 909090.

Talk to your doctor

Your doctor can help by prescribing antidepressants (these are not addictive) for a short time. Also, many surgeries now have counselling services available on the premises or can refer you for counselling or therapy.

If you've noticed other symptoms that seem to have occurred since the redundancy, such as headaches, migraine, other aches and pains, especially neck and back ache, cold or flu symptoms that seem to hang around but don't develop into anything much, or intestinal problems like stomach pains, indigestion, diarrhoea, mention these to your doctor. There are all sorts of stress-related conditions that require treatment to be given for the stress as well as medical diagnosis.

Looking after your health

Never forget to look after yourself! This applies to both partners and to the whole family. You need to try to stay as fit and healthy as you can in order to be able to manage the period without work as well as being ready to sparkle and shine at the interview that leads to the new one.

It's tempting when you're feeling down to comfort yourself with food and alcohol. Too much of either or both of these, though, will only make you feel worse about yourself and, ultimately, even more depressed than before.

Alcohol and depression

This is easy to say and well-known to be true, but, when you're in a depressed state of mind alcohol, particularly, plays tricks with your ability to reason. You find yourself thinking, 'Why *shouldn't* I have another pint?' Then, when you do, you feel guilty and cross with yourself for not having the strength of will to resist that little internal voice. So, you feel even more depressed because, apart from anything else, you know you can't afford it. Then, to comfort yourself, you have yet another pint! It's a real vicious circle.

Unless you know in your heart that you would be better to give up alcohol completely – which you might choose to do as a worthwhile part of your plan for the time you'll be out of work – then it may be more realistic to plan to cut down.

For anyone who loves and lives with someone who has, or seems to be developing a drink problem, finding a balance between helping and being supportive and criticizing or blaming – which is likely to have the opposite effect – is, quite frankly, immensely difficult.

If you or your partner needs help or advice about drinking too much, try calling Drinkline on 0171–332 0202 or there are alcohol advisory and counselling services listed in the telephone directory for your area.

Exercise

While you're 'between jobs', you suddenly have the time you may never have found before in which to get fit and take the exercise you know you should and need to take. If you're already a paid-up member of a sports club, don't immediately cancel your membership in the belief that it's a luxury you can do without. You need to exercise and can also enjoy the company of people you know there – some of whom will probably be on your networking list. So, when the subscription comes up for renewal next time, depending on your financial situation and the likely prospects for the next membership period, you may have to reassess the situation, but don't cancel it straight away. Even then, if things are tight, there may be other options – maybe you could become a daytime, weekday member at a lower charge or there may be reduced rates for the unwaged (don't be ashamed to ask about these).

Exercise doesn't need to be expensive. Keeping fit can be a matter of making a point of walking to the shops for the newspaper instead of taking the bus or the car. Making this walk slightly longer and walking briskly rather than ambling or strolling along will make it even more

GETTING HELP AND HELPING YOURSELF

beneficial! Indeed, walking is very good form of exercise and, now you have more time, you might like to make it an interest or hobby by joining other walkers to add extra interest and enjoyment to the pursuit. There is usually a local walking or rambling group (look in your local paper or check with the Ramblers Association, at: 1–5 Wandsworth Road, London SW8 2LX, Tel: 0171–582 6878/6826).

Aerobic exercise is supposed to be what we all need to do to keep ourselves healthy. Aerobics needn't mean leotards and expensive trainers and going to an expensive gym – it means any exercise that makes your heart beat faster and makes you puff! Turning that walk into a bit of a jog – as opposed to a run – is a perfectly acceptable form of aerobic exercise and free. Cycling is even better and cheap, too – as long as you don't have to go out and buy a bike! Swimming exercises the whole body and is aerobic. If you're a long way from the sea, swimming pools usually offer reduced rates for the unwaged.

Just making sure you get out of the house and walk purposefully somewhere is exercise and will, in itself, provide a break in a day that otherwise may threaten to become depressing.

8
Adjustments

Once you've been made redundant, your perceptions are changed overall. You take a much more personal and defensive view of the future. You look upon work as transient. Your attitude to money is changed. Money is used to service day-to-day things. You learn to make your money work for you. Your financial attitude to savings is completely different. You think on a day-to-day, short-term basis.

Alan

Alan was 32 when he was made redundant. He was a departmental manager with a sizeable staff. He received no warning about the redundancies his company was about to make and knew nothing about it until the day it happened. He was single at the time and had no children.

The day after he was made redundant, he remembers, 'everything was different'.

'How does it change you', I asked?

There is no cleansing effect. It makes you a more aware person and I think you're less trusting as a consequence. It's disquieting, especially if your life is based around your employment and you've chosen where you live because of your place of work. Your environment feels very unstable. Afterwards, you're always aware it could happen again. I noticed that when you've been made redundant, you tend to become a kind of counsellor or adviser to others when it happens to them, but there are no words of comfort.

When I met Alan, he had been in continuous employment, in a different branch of his previous field of work, for most of the ten years since he had been made redundant, but he had never lost the residual fear the experience had created. He did say, however, that, 'When you've been on both sides, you should be a better manager.'

John

John, on the other hand, who was in his late twenties when he was 'let go', has rather different feelings about his redundancy.

It all worked out for the best in the end. I'd never wanted to get stuck in the job I was in then and the job I have now is much better.

Had the redundancy affected the way he thought about money and the future?

No, it hasn't really. At first – in the first week, for instance – Vicky wanted to cancel a weekend away we'd planned for our first anniversary, but I didn't want to. In the end, by the end of that first week, I'd got the new job, so we celebrated both things!

The redundancy money was good and actually helped us when we wanted to move the following year. Just before I was made redundant, I'd taken out a pension and a savings scheme and we deliberately didn't take out a redundancy insurance when we bought the new flat. I actually have far more confidence in myself and my ability to get a new job, now, if it ever happens again.

In fact, John was head-hunted a year after taking up the first job after his redundancy and is now with a much bigger, international company, feeling even more confident and happy than before!

The day that changes your life

When you've been made redundant, you do change – you have to. And the people close to you have to be prepared to change and adapt, too. This is the *second* key to survival. Teamwork, the first, is essential, but the ability and preparedness to change and adapt is also absolutely vital.

The person who's lost their job and is out of work changes in various ways and over time. Both partners in the relationship have to recognize these changes and be prepared to make adjustments or alterations to attitudes, opinions, assumptions and the way the relationship works at virtually every level.

The Human Resource Manager, AG, said that often the problem is:

> the wife not being prepared to adapt. In many cases I've seen, it's been the wife who's been unable to bring herself to understand that the redundancy was anything but the husband's fault. She's perhaps been sympathetic for a couple of weeks and then started thinking, 'Why haven't you found anything yet? You can't be trying hard enough.'

After initial sympathy, it's quite easy for the partner whose life has also been overturned to become less understanding. Fear and uncertainty about the future can easily lead to anger directed at the person who seems to have caused the upset. Even Wendy, whose natural teamwork with Colin seemed solidly established, went through a wobbly time:

> After a while, things do begin to get on top of you. I'm not noted as a patient person. I like to be in control of my part of life, my own situation.

The job Colin had taken a week after his redundancy, as we have seen, proved to be a disaster, but whenever Wendy found something advertised in the newspaper that she felt Colin could apply for, he refused. They'd talked about the idea of him taking over 'her' business running the B&B, but Wendy wasn't keen. She didn't believe he could do it properly and by then she was thinking:

> I can't understand how he can sit in front of the TV when there's so many different things to be done.

It's easy to get tired of having to jolly someone along, and there's a limit to how long you can go on boosting your partner's confidence when your own is fraying at the edges the more worried you become. But this is a shared problem, so you have a right to discuss it and ask questions about matters that affect you and the family.

Living with the feelings

The problem with living with the results of a redundancy and a period of unemployment is that the feelings go very deep, for most people who experience it. Self-respect and confidence dives to rock bottom, and, if that's not bad enough, there's also a feeling of guilt for letting yourself and the family down. Your responses to feelings like these and your ability to deal with them depend on the person you are and your previous life experience. As AG said:

> If you're a fairly strong, together person, you're going to survive better, but if, underneath, you're a very insecure person who's been using the job as a prop, you're going to suffer.

And different people react differently to the effects of the emotional blow. For some, like John, it's not much more than a ripple, something that actually encouraged his belief in himself and his ability to survive in the workplace. For others, 'I think it's the shaking of confidence and the terrible feeling of rejection that can trail people along for ever', said AG, and continued:

> When I meet or come across people who've been made redundant or I look at applications from people who've been through redundancy, I've noticed that sometimes it isn't only once that it happens. It can become a terrible pattern. I think maybe something fatal was eroded

from them the first time around and then there's a sort of feeling of acceptance. So, the next time, when you know things are happening in your company or organization and other people are putting on their best face and fighting it and looking good, you've disappeared into a corner because you've already given up. Or there's a paranoia, from the beginning of a new job, that you're continually expecting your back to be stabbed.

The effects

There's certainly a need for work to be done on yourself when you've suffered redundancy. The effects of the feelings it can engender can be so damaging that they may colour your whole future.

You have to be prepared to look at yourself to see if there is, or was, something in you or your behaviour that may have contributed to the loss of your job in the first place. It's worth looking at your *reactions* to it as well, to see where they came from and if you need to do some rethinking and reassessment of yourself. If, as AG said, you realise that you were using your job as a prop to hold up your basic insecurity, you could work on rebuilding your self-confidence so that it becomes something more solid – more like hardcore than shifting sand!

Work can be a way of using elements of yourself that you were uncomfortable about showing in your personal life. The prison officer who could keep his natural aggression simmering away but under control when at work in the prison service, but who fell apart, became an emotional wreck and totally impotent when he was made redundant, is a sad example of this. He found work, eventually, as a bailiff, where he could, on occasion, legitimately go into homes where rent was unpaid and remove every stick of furniture and possessions. His potency returned with the recovery of employment.

Surviving redundancy can have worthwhile effects in terms of finding a new understanding of yourself. At some levels, though, it can be somewhat negative. For example, Michael feels that, for him:

> The overall effect is to make you cynical – or more cynical – especially if you value loyalty. People (i.e. employers) want you to be loyal without understanding that it's a two-way street. And it does affect your ability to go on and do it again. You're so certain that it's going to happen again, it almost becomes a self-fulfilling prophecy.
>
> When you get the kind of confidence boost I've had in the last year, you start feeling better about yourself again. [Michael had three long contracts with separate employers as an Interim Manager, for which he was selected in competition with others.] But you're always aware that you could be knocked back again.

ADJUSTMENTS

What Michael now says, is that:

> Once upon a time I believed I would starve unless I found a job doing what I think I'm good at. Now I know that I'm no longer what I was, but I am at least someone who can earn a living.

The bitter feelings of rejection that come as such a violent blow to a self-confidence which may be fairly thin is bound to reverberate in your life, probably for ever. But, if you can learn to deal with the feelings and learn from them, the strength and genuine confidence this will bring will also last for ever.

The risk is that the fears set up a self-defeating pattern, which Michael knows only too well. I have seen this happen more than once. It goes something like this:

- 'I've been offered a job.'
- 'But I won't be able to do what they want me to do. I won't be able to perform [that terrible word!] to the level of their expectations.'
- 'They won't like me or I won't be able to get on with people.'
- 'They'll get rid of me.'
- 'What shall I do next?'

Before such a person has even started a new assignment or a new job, they're planning how they'll get out of it and how they'll represent it on their CV!

However, if this person thinks it all through and has a chance to re-evaluate their life and career so far, they are at least aware of the pattern and can deal with the feelings as they come up.

The ex-husband of a friend of mine apparently developed a pattern of leaving every job he ever got after a few months because he said it wasn't working out. He said he was 'getting out before they pushed me out', but there'd been little evidence, my friend says, that anything was wrong, except his belief in himself. Eventually he 'got out' of his marriage in the same way and she divorced him.

Most of us have some deep-rooted insecurities that develop out of some of our earliest experiences. For example, someone who was useless at sports at school, always being one of the last to be chosen when teams were being selected, will, understandably, feel a little stab of fear whenever there is an element of 'choosing' in something they're doing. Even if they were the one always chosen by their classmates to be the form monitor all the way up the school and chosen as house captain and prefect in their final year makes not the slightest difference!

The fear of feeling stupid is incredibly powerful and, of course, this relates to the fear of feeling rejected or 'not good enough' once you feel you've been 'chosen' for redundancy.

Breaking the pattern

If you've suffered redundancy, but want to come back fighting, you have to be prepared and to find the courage to break this kind of self-defeating pattern. Otherwise the fears become crippling.

Both partners in a relationship need to be aware of these likely effects and the patterns that could be repeated. You have to develop the skill to see what's happening and draw the other's attention to it, without being seen as negative or unsupportive. A touch of humour can sometimes help in this or the gentle reminder that 'We've been here before' can just jog the memory, as well as recalling that we came through it before and can do so again.

Operating a sort of personal behaviour therapy can be very productive. A behaviour therapist 'cures' you of a phobia, such as a fear of spiders (arachnophobia), by helping you learn to control the way you *feel* when you see a spider. The therapist takes you through a series of stages of the feelings of terror. First, perhaps, by looking at a picture of a spider and ending up by holding a spider in your hand. In a similar way, you can train yourself to cope with the feelings of fear – or the patterns of self-destructive thinking – that occur when you've had your belief in yourself shattered by being ready for the triggers that set off the pattern of feelings and knowing that you can go through them without falling apart.

To take an everyday example of how this can be done, if you get uptight before setting off on a journey, panicking that you'll forget something crucial, like the tickets or your passport, or miss the train or flight, knowing that you have this hang-up can help you deal with it. You can take deep breaths or a herbal calming tablet and get on with it. You can make lists, leave an extra half an hour earlier to get to the station or airport and so on as precautions against the outcome you fear. If you let fear control you – or what you do with your life – you will end up disappointed and frustrated or, worse still, 'bitter and twisted'.

Shared lessons and making adjustments

As we have seen, there are lessons to be learned from the reactions you've both had to the redundancy. Because you're intent on surviving as a couple and as a team, it's important to be aware of each other's feelings and sensitive to them. But, at the same time, it's important to understand that you cannot feel what the other is feeling, nor can you 'make it better' for each other.

Life, and certainly a long-term relationship, involve an endless process of adjustment. Nothing stays the same because circumstances and situations change all the time, mostly while we're unaware of it. Sometimes we can adjust to changes without really being aware of doing so. We adjust to changes in our relationship with our children, for instance, as they grow up. On their eighteenth birthday, you find yourself looking back and wondering how it all happened so fast, when it seemed as if they'd never get through all the stages between being a toddler and a teenager, let alone those beyond.

In a vibrant relationship, both partners develop and change as time goes on, but they keep pace with each other and value each other's differences. In a relationship that is stagnant, though, any alteration to the status quo is likely to cause ripples or waves and these may threaten to throw it against the rocks. So, the strength of the existing relationship is crucial to how you survive such a major alteration in the family's circumstances as redundancy. And the ability of both partners to adapt to all the changes in each other and in themselves and to be prepared to contribute in a different way, perhaps, to the ways they did before the redundancy – in an unselfish way, but, of course, in the interests of them both – is essential.

Sacrifices may need to be made – big ones and smaller ones, such as the following.

Moving to find work

One major change might be that the whole family needs to be uprooted and move to where a new job is located. This is a real possibility for people in more specific areas of employment who are unable or unwilling to change direction in their career as they have to go where the work is. For their families this can, of course, be a problem, especially if close family, such as elderly parents, have to be left behind. Children, too, can find that their progress at school is disrupted if they're moved at a crucial time, say when they've begun their coursework for exams.

Michael Witcher feels strongly about the impact GCSE courses have on the ability of parents to be mobile in terms of their employment and career. He believes that no one at the Department of Education has made the connection between parents being unwilling to up sticks and move and the fact that their children's education is at a crucial stage. This factor affects families at around the time most parents are between the ages of 30 and 40, which is the age at which many employees face redundancy.

The 1994 Client Family Survey, an annual research project undertaken by Drake Beam Morin, found that over 50 per cent of partners of those who'd been made redundant *would* be prepared to move if this would improve the prospects of finding a new job for the chief wage earner in the family. However, if the partner who had been made redundant was *female*, only 12 per cent of their male partners would consider relocating in her favour. Not a particularly surprising finding!

If relocating is a serious possibility, therefore, then it is a matter that must be discussed by the whole family. A great deal of discussion and preparation needs to be done, both with the children themselves and with their teachers at the present and new schools to try to reduce the disruption as much as possible. A positive aspect of a move for children can be that they learn to be more adaptable and make friends in a new school, which could be a worthwhile development for their future. Indeed, Michael Witcher believes that the concept that employees need to be prepared to change and adapt throughout their working lives should already be starting in schools.

Working away from home

Many couples are used to the idea of their men working away from home, sometimes for months at a time. Partners of men in the armed forces or of offshore oil workers, for example, get used to the special problems of regular separations. But, if a man finds that, after redundancy, he can only earn his living again by working too far away from home to return each night, learning to adapt to this new situation can cause problems. Things can go wrong, as in the case of Neil and Sarah.

Neil and Sarah

Neil had worked as a technician in the Midlands since he was 16. He married the girl next door, Sarah, they had two children, and, for 12 years, they had a happy, stable family life.

Their home was a nicely kept three-bedroom semi and, most years, they managed to do some DIY improvements to it, as well as having a couple of weeks' holiday. Life was pretty comfortable – until the day the company Neil worked for folded and he found himself out of work.

For 18 months, Neil tried to get work, without success. He was on the point of giving up when he saw an advertisement for a technician's job in West Sussex. After talking it over with Sarah, he decided to apply for the job.

Three weeks later, he started. The fact that he would have to move South to live in a bedsit until their house could be sold didn't deter him – he had a job and he was elated! They decided that Sarah and the children would stay in their house until it was sold, then they'd move down to be with Neil.

Nearly a year later, the house was still on the market – only three people had viewed it and the price had been reduced twice. Neil got home only once every six weeks as finances were stretched because they now had to pay the mortgage *and* the rental of his bedsit.

One Sunday, Neil received a phone call from his sister telling him to come home because his wife was seeing another man. When he confronted her, Sarah didn't deny it. She said she was depressed and lonely with Neil away, but she still loved him, so they decided to put this behind them.

Sarah came down the following week, with the children, and, for three weeks, they lived in the cramped bedsit. The landlady wasn't happy with this situation and neither was Sarah, who said she'd go back home, reduce the price of the house still further or let it so that she could come back to be with Neil. Reluctantly, Neil agreed.

Three weeks later, Neil received a letter from Sarah asking for a divorce. She said she couldn't stand the strain any more. The new man in her life was kind to her and the children and she was going to live with him.

Neil still works in West Sussex and has bought a flat. Not surprisingly, he's bitter about his redundancy, which he sees as not only having cost him his job, but his home, his wife and his children.

This is a sad story and maybe the outcome could have been avoided if Neil and Sarah had, perhaps, been different people and if they had at least tried, perhaps with counselling help, to find a way through the situation.

Some partners find that their relationships are actually *enhanced* by separation.

Gina and Peter

Gina is used to long periods of time apart from her husband Peter. An offshore oil worker, he's worked away regularly for the last 20 years. Gina says:

At first, I used to get really upset, but now I think I'm lucky. When Peter's away, I can be my own person, do my own thing and not feel guilty about it. It's also made me want to get any problems in our relationship sorted out, rather than let things drift, because our time together is so precious.

Gina, among other activities, now runs a support network for partners, families and friends of workers like her husband. Gina is a perfect example of someone who, because she wanted to enough, made a difficult, problematical situation work both for herself and for her marriage.

ADJUSTMENTS

The effects on the extended family

Sometimes adjustment needs to come from the wider family – grandparents and other relatives, as well as friends and neighbours.

Michael

> Michael, looking back, felt that his own mother was concerned about his first redundancy and a later long period of unemployment and was encouraging in her way. His father-in-law, on the other hand, was very critical, and Michael felt that he thought Michael had let his daughter down. They argued frequently, which, to be fair, was not a new situation, but didn't help Michael's deteriorating relationship with his wife.

Wendy said she was surprised, in retrospect, that Colin's parents hadn't seemed to be more affected by Colin's redundancy:

> Perhaps they were too busy, but I'd have thought they'd have been on the phone every other day, asking how we were doing, and they weren't.

Involve your own parents and in-laws if you want to, but not if you don't. How you feel will depend on the relationship you have with them! Some might be useful as part of your network of contacts, helping you in your search for work, but others are, perhaps, best left in ignorance, after you've reassured them that you're managing and coping.

A sense of shame

If you feel a sense of shame or embarrassment, for instance, when talking to friends and neighbours, or come up against the classic situation at a party when you meet someone you don't know and they ask, 'What do you do?', it may be wise to find a phrase or expression you feel comfortable with to describe your present situation. You might think this through and be prepared in advance with:

- 'I'm between jobs at present and I'm rethinking my life.'
- 'I'm planning a new career.'
- 'I'm working on an evaluation of my next move.'

These days, it is probably best never to ask that question. If you want to know, you can find out in a more subtle way, by turning the conversation to, for instance, how you happen to be at the same party or where you live.

ADJUSTMENTS

Surviving redundancy and going through a period of unemployment inevitably alters the way you see yourself, your family and your future, but, by being open to change and making the necessary adjustments, it is possible to come through the experience having learned some useful lessons.

9
Positive thinking

The first positive thought anyone can have after they've been made redundant is 'I am not alone'. It may *feel* like you *are* alone at first, and, of course, your situation, like you, is unique, but the fact is that more and more people are losing their jobs as the national economy, the global economy and the development of technology affects the world of work.

The changing world of work

The future for work will be different from what we have known so far. AG, with her professional experience of human resource management and her personal experience of having been made redundant twice, says:

> People have got to be very lateral. We all have to start thinking about taking two or three part-time jobs, which I do believe is probably the way forward now for all of us as things are changing so much.
>
> You have to change the whole way you think about work. When I started work (in the early 1960s), the whole thing was loyalty to your employer. But, somehow, now we've got to get rid of that. You can't afford to think, 'I'll do whatever they ask me because I owe them loyalty' because you don't! You owe what you're *contracted* to do and no more because that is all you'll get from them. But, to try and change the way you think is . . . very hard.

Michael Witcher and, indeed, every other professional in the field of human resources and recruitment we talked to, agrees that now 'there's no such thing as a job for life.'

> Now you have to expect to change jobs several times during a 30 to 40-year career span. And you have to plan with this in mind. If you're in work, you've got to be planning for the next job – adding new skills and new qualifications.
>
> It's about the individual taking on board the management of their own career and having a very proactive attitude. Being aware of objectives which will change over time and what changes are needed. And, whether they're 20 or 50 years old, taking on new skills and new competences to make them suitable for the market out there.

Another positive thought is the one we've mentioned before – that *you* aren't made redundant, your *job* or *position* is. As one of the personnel managers we spoke to reported:

> There's a statistic that's now been produced, showing that the fact of whether you're good at your job or not is only of about 20 per cent importance in how you're actually judged and perceived in the workplace. The rest is personality and how you get on with other staff.

So, it's necessary for all of us to be aware of the impermanence of work and the possibility of losing our jobs – whatever they are and whoever you are. It's a hard fact of life and one that, as Michael says, encourages cynicism, but at least if you are in some way prepared, you can consciously develop a variety of skills, as well as a wide network of contacts, ready for any eventuality!

Planning your come-back

If the redundancy can be seen as a new chance to find new work that might be better and more fulfilling than the old job, then the time between jobs is a chance to plan and plot for the opportunities ahead.

If there is no realistic option but to find new employment, then at least there is the chance to take stock of yourself and reassess and re-present yourself on the job market. Certainly this is an area where both partners can contribute to the thinking.

Laying the ghosts to rest

If the partner who has been made redundant has been plagued by misery and depression since the loss of the job, then positive thinking in this case means taking a positive approach to rethinking attitudes and making a real attempt to break patterns that only hold back and restrict. It may mean resolving to seek help from a counsellor or therapist to help you or your partner break free and recover.

Making the most of being out of work

Much has been written in the years of recession about redundancy and unemployment and how to find a new job. More recently, there has been more awareness that a period of time out of work can have very considerable positive effects on your life and the way you approach it.

For a couple, the whole experience can become an opportunity to become closer together, fighting a common enemy, when, before, perhaps you've been drifting along, not taking too much notice of each other, just getting along in a superficial sort of a way.

Denise Knowles, spokesperson for Relate, when I met her and colleagues in Northampton, said:

> Sometimes people re-evaluate everything after the loss of a job. Sometimes they find they can think about doing something they've always dreamed of, like selling the house in Northampton and moving to the coast of Spain or opening a café or restaurant or running a B&B business using the rooms the children used when they lived at home . . . or anything!
>
> But, first, there has to be acknowledgement that one part of life has ended and the next part is just beginning. Once you've done that, you can begin to look at redundancy as an opportunity – a chance to live a dream.

Not having to go out to work every day is certainly a magnificent opportunity to look at yourself, what you've done with your life so far and see what you'd like to do in the future. You've time to learn something you've always wanted to learn or do something you've always wanted to try. As a couple, you have a chance to spend time together that you could not have done while one or both of you was going out to work.

Some of what you may wish to do may cost money and, for most people who are out of work, this is an issue. However, even the chance to talk about what you'd like to do and planning how you could do it is, in itself, a kind of opportunity.

Re-evaluating your relationship

As Relate counsellors have found, some couples re-evaluate their relationships only to decide that what they have is not what they want. The new situation just will not work or they allow the drastic change in circumstances to break their marriage apart. Others find that they are stronger together than before.

Again, counselling can be used as a way of refreshing your relationship and enhancing it. To this end, there are several 'refresher courses for couples', such as Rapport (see Useful addresses) and specific religion-based groups, which set up day or residential weekend seminars at locations around the country. On such courses, couples can rethink and refine their communication and care for each other in a safe and unthreatening environment. There are fees for such courses, which some partners might see as an investment in their relationship.

Relate is the most well-known source of help with relationships, but there are other reputable and reliable relationship counselling agencies, such as those affiliated to the Westminster Pastoral Foundation, and services, such as the Catholic Marriage Advisory Council (which is for anyone of any denomination), and other, more specific counselling and advisory services, such as the Jewish Marriage Council and the Asian Family Counselling Service (see the Useful addresses section at the end of the book for details).

Some people look for a helpful book as a first source of help and advice in any given situation. Others prefer the DIY approach or talking to someone face to face. If you *do* find books helpful, a good place to start is the series of Relate Guides, and, in this instance, particularly *The Relate Guide to Better Relationships* by Sarah Litvinoff (Vermilion, 1991).

As there's no doubt that the way to survive is to work together, it's a worthwhile exercise for both partners to look at the relationship to see if there are areas that could be improved and problems that need sorting out. This can only help the survival process and will stand you in good stead for the future.

Coping with working away from home

If the only option has been for the partner who was made redundant to find work away from home, positive thinking will help the one who's left behind to manage the home and family.

As with many things in life, the first time is always the worst. You're worried you'll be lonely and will be managing all the things that can go wrong, while, at the same time, your partner's worrying both about leaving you and about the new job. Don't try to pretend you're perfectly calm. Talk about your feelings and anxieties and ask for reassurance from each other.

After the first time, it will get better! Separations, handled well, can enrich a relationship. They can boost your confidence that you can manage alone and make you appreciate each other more – and making up for lost time when your partner comes back home can be like a mini-honeymoon!

If you have small children, the time your partner's away can be marked off on a calendar, which they can make into a learning experience as well as being a way to help them understand. Very young children can take quite a time to remember who the person returning is, but patience and calm reassurance will help restore things to normal.

Older children might become difficult both at home and at school. Giving them some responsibility in the house might help, as well as reminding them of the reasons your partner has to work. Getting too heavy handed is a mistake, as is using the absent parent as a threat of punishment when they return – turning them into a kind of demon figure is unfair and dangerous.

Keeping in regular contact with your partner by telephone and letters is fun for both the children and the absent parent and can be a regular weekly project. When they come home again, be aware of the risks of becoming defensive and 'territorial'. If you've found you can cope with organizing the family all by yourself and quite enjoy the confidence it gives you, be prepared to let your partner take over the reins again when they come back – if that's what they're used to and what they want. If your partner's not threatened by your new-found capabilities, they'll be proud of you!

Keeping hope alive

If, like Colin, you take the first job that comes up and then regret it, the only way of coping is to hang on to the knowledge that it's paying the bills and keeping a roof over your heads, while trying to think again about the future. Wendy told me that she remembered that Michael had advised caution when we first met them the day after Colin's redundancy. She said:

> It's not easy advice to take. We were so frightened and the offer seemed like a good chance. Colin thought quite a lot of the man who gave him the job, at the time, but he turned out to be an A1 idiot!

In the end, they listed contacts and companies he could approach in the field of products Colin had been selling in before, so, when the dreadful job came to an end, they were ready.

For many people, the search for a job goes on for weeks, months and even years. For them, keeping hope alive is an act of faith and it's often an enormous burden for their partners. But as AG says:

> Sometimes I don't think people understand quite how hard you've got to work to get a job again. I see letters saying I've applied for 110 jobs and I've got nothing – 110 job applications is nothing!
>
> I do believe in the advice given by outplacement counsellors and books about redundancy, that if you're out of work you've got to get up at the normal time and you've got to put on your work clothes – not your casual clothes because that puts a different attitude in your mind – and you've got to work at it for a whole office day. Give yourself weekends off, as usual, but work from 9 to 5.

And do every single speculative letter you can think of. The number of people this organization takes on because of spec letters is actually quite high. I came here myself because of a speculative approach, and I got my last job the same way. It really does work!

It's just the 'window of opportunity'. In 99 times out of 100, it's the wrong time – but that *one* time you can write to an organization just when they are thinking of taking on someone. It's very, very important. And networking is terribly important, too, although it can be very hard to do at the time when you're feeling so desperately downcast.

Speaking as someone who interviews and selects candidates for a large, national organization and has considerable previous experience – along with personal experience of being made redundant, twice – AG's views are based on fact – and are passionate!

If you're an ordinary person, looking for an ordinary job and you reply to an advertisement, you're probably up against 500 other people and you have to be something very special. Nobody's looking to see what sort of person you are, they're just seeing if you fit those predetermined criteria – and there's nothing you can do about that. So, any sort of introduction or contact is worth so much. You have to use Jobclubs or any sort of network you can get into . . . and maybe you still won't be lucky.

She believes it's unnecessary to hide a redundancy on a CV and she herself says:

It doesn't necessarily mean that I wouldn't want to see that person because I also understand, having been through it myself, that if you take on someone who's suffered a redundancy, they're so pleased to be back at work and so grateful for the chance, that, my goodness you get a lot out of them! But, you do have to be aware that you have to be much gentler with them as well.

A long, drawn-out search for employment is incredibly draining on the one who's out of work and on their partner. It's survival of the fittest! But here are two examples of determined people.

Each day I get up and tell myself 'This could be the day the right job comes along'. I know my CV is honest and well-presented, my letter's just right, and I have a good telephone manner. I'm an excellent administrator, good at statistics, with excellent interpersonal skills.

POSITIVE THINKING

I have been trained as a personnel/human resource manager, a community worker and, since I returned to my home town, I have experience in the quarrying industry. I have been a sales office supervisor and run a transport department. My ambition is to manage a quarry, or as near to that as is realistic. I'm working hard to find a position in this industry and my efforts will be rewarded when the right company replies.

In the meantime, I've drawn on my personnel experience and have managed to find odd weeks' work as cover for Jobclub leaders and Jobplan tutors. This isn't every week, but it keeps me mentally alert and earns me some money. I continue my job search even during the weeks I work.

I just refuse to believe that I am never going to have a permanent job again. I know I can give a great deal to a company.

This young lady deserved a chance and we can only hope that since she wrote this letter, she has been given it. If not, someone needs to help her to channel all that determination and energy towards a variation on or another part of the quarrying industry she's so hooked on.

Now to our second determined person.

I have been unemployed for over a year now and, as time goes by, I am feeling a bit better about myself. That is, I've learned to accept the failures rather than just the successes.

Despite some personal illness, I have tried to look at what is happening around me. I try to understand the meaning and, more importantly, to laugh when things go wrong.

Having worked through many career plans and changes, I sometimes end up wondering if it's worth planning for the future. But then I think, there is always light at the end of the tunnel.

I've taken up creative writing and only now have I found that I have a gift of imagination, so at last I have something to keep my mind active. I hope that I may even be able to make a living out of it one day.

I hope that other readers will look at my experience, no matter how bad things are, and maybe they will discover in themselves things they are good at that they've never been aware of.

10
Solutions and resolutions

When we talked to Wendy, six months after Colin had lost his job, she said, rather fiercely, 'If I was reading a book like the one you're writing, I'd want answers!' Later on, she compared this response with the way she felt when her youngest son, Robin, had been diagnosed with a quite serious blood complaint. He'd been ill for a while and doctors seemed confused as to what was causing the problem. When the condition was diagnosed, Wendy said she had wanted answers from the doctors to this problem. She wanted to know what was to be done and who would do it, so that he would get better.

Wendy, as she says herself, is not noted for her patience and she's a practical, energetic person who gets things done, but I knew what she meant about the book and I'm sure many other people, when faced with redundancy for the first time, feel just the same. Others, perhaps of a less practical nature, want comfort first of all and then ideas and suggestions.

In counselling training, there are valid arguments against using a directive approach with people and so we felt obliged to say to Wendy that there could never be black and white answers to her situation – or, indeed, to any other couple's – because everyone is unique and everyone wants a different solution. All we can do is offer suggestions based on experience and the experience of many other people, both personal and professional, and hope that some ideas can be found from these.

Solutions

There are, of course, as many solutions to the problem of redundancy when it is faced by a couple as there are couples! As AG said:

> If people know what the pitfalls [of being out of work] are – if they want to work at it – they can. *But don't let anybody think it's going to be an easy ride, because it isn't!*
>
> But you'll find families who say that because they've been through redundancy, they've emerged as a stronger unit. And you read stories about people who've given up very stressful jobs and are doing something that gives them a lot of satisfaction – not much money, but a lot of satisfaction!

SOLUTIONS AND RESOLUTIONS

Some real-life stories

Bill

Bill was a designer with an aircraft company, one of the first to be made redundant when the market for turbo-prop aircraft first collapsed. When several of his colleagues saw the writing on the wall, they chose to leave 'before they were pushed'. As a result, Bill's notice was withdrawn and he stayed on for another three years before finally being made redundant.

He turned to woodcarving, one of his previous leisure activities and, before long, found his work much in demand. His greatest regret in later life was not having taken redundancy earlier. He was able to work from home, with no fares for commuting. He could work hours to suit himself and his grandchildren and every marketing trip was combined with shopping and sightseeing. No doubt he forgot about the apparent loss of social standing when he was elected Commodore of the local yacht club!

Dennis

Dennis was an architect. He'd had a quiet, undemanding career, but when his firm went under in the mid 1980s and he was made redundant, it seemed like a disaster. His children had arrived late and were still young, so his wife took on a full-time job, using her skills in information technology.

Dennis had always enjoyed drawing and a neighbour asked him to do a line drawing of his house in Islington, north London. Someone else saw this and, before he knew it, Dennis was overwhelmed with requests for the delicate, architectural drawings of Georgian and Victorian buildings he was producing.

The irony of this success story is that, after a couple of years, Dennis was asked to join a friend who was setting up a small, new architects' group, so he's gone back into architecture just when he should have been retiring!

One of the happiest stories Clare Stronge and Michael Witcher told was of the young woman in her early thirties who was an employee at a factory that was closing down.

Both her parents had died tragically in an accident just as she was about to take O levels. She hadn't sat the exams, but, instead, had taken a temporary job in a retail store.

Later, she'd drifted into various factories and on to the shop floor. She was a very, very angry person and pretty screwed up, Michael remembered, when she attended their outplacement counselling seminars.

SOLUTIONS AND RESOLUTIONS

A series of aptitude and psychometric tests confirmed her basic potential and that she was in the MENSA top 5 per cent of the population – 'And she'd been in a factory, packing boxes!' Michael exclaimed.

She showed an interest in computers and, because the factory closure was classed as a 'mass redundancy', she was able to take a free place on a six-month course at the local college of further education to study information technology straight away.

Clare Stronge says:

> She enjoyed every minute of the course and it not only gave her the skills and qualifications she wanted but also gave her so much more confidence in herself. She's now in a permanent job working in shipping and export. It's taking a while for her to settle in because of the enormous difference between working on a factory floor and working in an office, but she feels now that the sky's the limit!

An obvious success story, and one that might not have happened at all if the factory in which she had been employed had not closed down!

Another happy outcome, from what was a potentially disastrous beginning, was the story of the man in his late forties who was made redundant in another factory closure. He was a fork-lift truck driver.

He had only been back at work for a few months, having recovered from a minor stroke that had affected his memory slightly. His wife was registered blind and her elderly mother, who lived with them, was bedridden and incapacitated. Since the stroke, this man had put on a lot of weight.

Michael Witcher, when he first talked with him about his future and his hopes for a new job, suggested that, as a start, he could 'look the part' by losing some weight and looking fitter. He asked the man's wife to come in and join the meeting. They talked about how he could improve his fitness by taking gentle exercise and thinking about what he ate and drank. His wife took this project on with enthusiasm and was determined to help and encourage her husband. They were an excellent team! 'The wife had a brain on her like a razor,' remembered Michael, and she was able to help her husband, who couldn't remember things as well since the stroke.

Together, they reassessed the family's position, in terms of State benefits, and looked at the sort of job the man might apply for. He lost a bit of weight, felt much happier and eventually found another job as a fork-lift driver. Teamwork in action!

Wendy and Colin's teamwork has also been operating successfully. After more than six months of dragging himself to the job at the garden centre and hating every minute of it, Colin had begun to think he'd have to look for something else. Wendy said:

> At that time we did what we should have done the last time. We drew up a list of names and addresses of companies Colin would like to work for and had some respect for. Then we composed a letter saying that, for the last few months, Colin had been working for Company X, but he would like to get back to the work he was good at, enjoyed and was successful at. We sent these letters off, received two or three acknowledgements, and one company wrote back and asked him to send his CV.
>
> We quickly put a new CV together, returned it and the Sales Director was on the telephone the next day!
>
> Colin went along and met him and was offered a six-month contract to cover an employee's maternity leave.
>
> It's a sales job, with a car, very similar to the job he had before, but with a much wider range of products to sell. Obviously it's only for six months and there's no guarantee of anything after that, but the Sales Director implied that there was a fair chance the employee might not return to work after her maternity leave.

When we talked, Wendy was obviously delighted. The news had come at a very good time, just as their youngest son had been declared almost recovered from the illness they'd been so worried about, and 'Colin's back to being a man again!', laughed Wendy.

Colin and Wendy will always be a good team – they complement each other well and seem to do almost everything they do together. If your relationship isn't already like that, you may have problems.

AG told me of a man who worked for the same organization as herself. He had been very ill with a brain tumour, which turned out to be benign. After eight months, he was back at work, but while he was ill, his wife was made redundant.

For a year, she has been trying to find work and, so far, she's been unsuccessful. She's tried retraining, she's tried everything, but the fracturing of the marriage is coming from his side.

He's all right now – he's back at work and OK and he isn't at all interested in the fact that finding work is such a problem for her. He earns about £20,000 and he thinks that while he's prepared to keep her, it should be enough for her to stay at home. He simply cannot understand how she's driven to say, 'I wish he'd died, then I'd have some money from the life insurance and I'd be able to go out and do something.'

Redundancy certainly shows up the cracks in a relationship and it's undoubtedly showing them up in this one. Without knowing the whole circumstances of this couple, this seems to be an example of a marriage where the balance has been upset and the husband, at least, seems to be unable to adapt to a new one. While he was extremely ill, he lost control and power and was totally dependent on his wife and on his doctors. He was able to accept this reversal of the status quo while he was ill, but he fails to understand why his wife cannot continue to concentrate on 'looking after him' now that he's better and that she wants to re-establish her own life by finding employment. It does not seem as if he is able to care for her in the way she was prepared to care for him when he was ill. Couples *can* succeed in working together, upturning the balance and keeping going after suffering the loss of an income, as Phil's story shows.

Phil

Phil went to sea in the Merchant Navy when he was 16, after O levels. He did well and rose to the rank of first mate, then, suddenly, the shipping company decided to cut staff and Phil received his redundancy notice, together with a substantial severance payment.

He wrote to every other shipping company he could find and, with 100 per cent refusals, he became angry and depressed.

When his girlfriend suggested he became a mature student and do a degree, he thought she was being silly or that he'd have to do A levels first, but he was surprised and pleased to be offered a place on a polytechnic course. He took it gratefully, but with trepidation. He used his redundancy pay-off to help fund his way through college and his girlfriend, who by then had become his wife, helped out.

Like many other mature students, Phil completed his course and gained a first class degree. He's been happily and successfully employed in a land-based career ever since and now sees his redundancy as a heaven-sent opportunity to change his life.

We have heard many other stories with happy endings in the process of writing this book, which give encouragement and hope for anyone for whom being out of work is a new experience.

Michael Witcher gave us one such good example, that of a woman who'd been a victim of mass redundancy in the company she'd worked for as the Print Room Manager.

She came to the seminar and then made an appointment for a personal consultation with Clare Stronge. When it was suggested to her that she could put her considerable experience into setting up and running a small business of her own using the same principles as those she had been using to operate the print room, she was amazed. With advice about small business grants and loans, lots of encouragement and her own energy, she found herself with her own company and was soon an employer herself!

For some people, redundancy can be a chance to try out a plan they'd perhaps thought of or dreamed about, but never before had an opportunity to put into practice, as we found when we met Bill and Irene.

Bill and Irene

Bill and Irene spent the early part of their marriage living in the South East. He was a building surveyor and she a primary school teacher who'd given up full-time work when their second child had been born disabled.

When Bill was made redundant, after 25 years with a large, international company, he decided that he wouldn't look for employment, but would start his own business.

They preferred staying in small bed and breakfast accommodation rather than impersonal hotels and, for several summers, they'd enjoyed holidays in the Lake District, so they decided to sell the family home and start a business in that part of the country.

They were lucky to find a buyer for their house within a couple of months. As this happened at the beginning of the summer, they bought an old caravan, packed it up and set off for Cumbria. They took a long time looking at property before they finally found the Georgian hunting lodge they have now, which is set in a beautiful valley not far from Kendal.

They renovated the house and converted some outbuildings into self-catering holiday apartments. The business seems to be successful and, certainly, Bill and Irene seem happily content.

Is age a problem?

There's no reason for you to be considered 'too old' to be re-employed or to find work if you're made redundant in your late forties or later. Certainly, you may have to think rather differently and be a little more lateral in your approach to new work, but, in fact, there is a movement among employers towards rethinking their policies regarding age. Indeed, in September 1995, an attempt was made to include ageism among laws against discrimination.

The DIY superstore company B&Q was far ahead of the field in its thinking when, in 1989, it decided to open a store in Macclesfield and staff it completely with people over 50 years old. This was swiftly followed by another similar store in Exmouth.

B&Q had found that staff turnover was very high, partly because the majority of their staff, up until that time, had been young. By employing more mature people, B&Q thought that it could address this problem and benefit in other ways, too. The Chairman and Chief Executive, Jim Hodkinson, said:

> Older people are more likely to be homeowners and to have done DIY themselves. Therefore, their knowledge and interest in DIY and DIY products is likely to be higher than in younger age groups.
>
> More mature employees are likely to have a different perspective on what constitutes good customer service and we often find that they spend more time with customers, helping them with their DIY queries.

Michael Witcher said of the project:

> These older employees brought experience, more staying power and enthusiasm, and the experiment proved highly successful.

B&Q was so pleased with the project, and, no doubt, the publicity it received, that it has developed the idea in all its stores. The company now no longer considers it necessary to maintain a solely over 50 policy at these stores, though, accepting that a store staffed with people of a mixture of ages, experience and backgrounds offers good-quality customer service. However, B&Q does not enforce retirement. Employees are given the opportunity to work after the age of 60 on a fixed-term contract and the company has employed staff as old as 80!

In August 1995, the company's development and growth had encouraged it to recruit experienced retail managers. Advertisements in national and trade press for people over 50 with these qualifications elicited 5,000 responses! Undoubtedly, this massive response also reflects the number of people of this age group who have been made redundant and are competing for employment, but someone has to get the job!

Clare Stronge remembers a man of 59, a stock controller, who came to her and told her that no one would want him. She sat him down, made him appreciate what he had done with his life so far, his work and skills, and helped him construct a new CV. She then put him in touch with all the local agencies in the area. Quite soon, a job came up and, with Clare's encouragement, he went along and got it.

The employer told Clare that, 'He'd much rather have him than a 20-year old who'll disappear in a couple of years'. That's not to say that *all* 20-year olds are going to be turned down in favour of people nearing retirement age, but it is also true that there are far too many young people desperately looking for work who haven't even been given a chance to gain experience that they can sell. Remember, though, that you're not written off and will never find work again once you're over 45.

Michael

Michael feared that this was the case at one point. There was a time when he was sending out his CV and deliberately leaving off his date of birth!

Having first been made redundant at the age of 43 and going through the next 6 years with short-term, unfortunate periods of employment and a year-long period of unemployment in between, his confidence and self-respect were at rock bottom, while his anxiety and stress levels were sky-high! If he was short-listed for interviews, he was either so laid back that he gave the impression he was bored and disinterested or he was so hyped up he appeared to be arrogant and overbearing. He found himself telling managing directors where they'd made their mistakes in the business so far and what they should have done instead.

Twice he was included in a final short list of two candidates, only to be turned down when the other one was chosen. You'd have thought that on the days those rejection letters landed on the doormat he'd have found it all just too much, but, somehow, he kept going and, once he knew he could come through the darkest moments of despair and out the other side, he would recover within a few days.

It was a chance meeting with a neighbour, during tea break while attending an evening class at the local college, that led to a lucky break and a series of interlocking interim management contracts.

His neighbour's husband was Regional Managing Director of a large housebuilder, who had come across Michael in the small world of the construction industry. He offered Michael the job of organizing a big promotional relaunch of his company's range of houses, which was to take place the following summer. Michael had never considered 'event management' as part of his skills portfolio, but, typically, he threw himself into the project with enthusiasm and, despite many problems and much hassle, it was an enormous success.

His disappointment was just as enormous, however, when, after all the compliments he received for his work, the company did not offer him another contract or, what he was hoping for, a full-time job.

Looking back, though, he found he'd recovered some of his belief in himself and his ability to do a good job, so, although it didn't happen immediately, when he was offered the first of a series of interim management contracts, he was more prepared for what was involved than he might have been before.

A year later, he answered an advertisement in the trade publication he'd always subscribed to and scanned each week. He was interviewed at length by the consultant the company had hired for the task of recruiting someone to be the General Manager for a small housebuilder in the Home Counties and then short-listed. After an interview with the Managing Director, he found himself in the last three being considered for the position, and the recruitment consultant said that he was 'by far the best qualified'. He got the job.

Michael changed, developed and, indeed, mellowed since his first redundancy. Especially during the year he was out of work, he was able to look at himself and his life up to that time and reassess himself. He had the courage to take an objective look at the way he behaved with people, especially with men, in a business and working relationship and found the strength to make changes. He is now a happier person!

What if there is no new employer?

Throughout this book there's been a tendency to assume that the redundancy and possible period without work will eventually be followed by a new job and new employer. It may be, though, that from choice or due to chance you are never employed again. You might become self-employed, set up your own small business working from home or work as part of a group project helping small businesses to get off the ground.

AG talked of HRH The Prince of Wales' Prince's Youth Trust, which sponsors various projects helping young people, and those who've been helped have found that it's 'changed their lives and [they] are doing what they want to do. It's the way forward!'

She also told me about the Custard Factory in Birmingham, a project set up in the old Bird's Custard factory, which has been converted into 140 units:

> There's some fantastic work going on there. It's all been made into little workshops now and a lot of unemployed people have started their own businesses. They have the support of others in the same situation, so there isn't the terrible loneliness of starting to make lemonade in their garden shed. It's absolutely incredible and very affirming to see what people can do!

Michael always said that because he spent a lot of time as a child with his grandfather, who was retired, he always knew how to occupy himself without work! He felt this was a disadvantage, in the sense that he should have been more actively engaged in the pursuit of employment, but it did mean that he was never bored or could find nothing to do. The garden pond would probably not have been designed and built had he not had a whole summer out of work!

There is always a great deal for those who don't have to go out to work to do. Whole organizations, such as the Abbeyfield Homes for the elderly, are run at local and regional level by small groups of people who give their time voluntarily, and charity shops are staffed in a similar way.

If you are not already involved with any sort of local voluntary project, the place to go to find out what's going on and where help is needed is your local Council for Voluntary Service or Volunteer Bureau (you'll find them in your telephone directory).

There's no doubt that getting involved in something worth while on a voluntary basis is a very positive way of rebuilding shattered self-esteem and making you feel better about yourself.

A chance to change

When your whole life is turned upside down, the most positive way to look at the resulting shambles is that it can be a marvellous chance to rearrange and reorder it all! Being put out of work can be a chance to change yourself, your relationship and your life for the better – or for the worse. The choice is yours.

Appendix:
The danger signs

- Are orders down?
- Has the company made a loss?
- Has the organization been taken over?
- Has a new boss been appointed?
- Has there been adverse press comment about the company or its management?

Keeping your eyes and ears open

In most cases, redundancy shouldn't come as a complete surprise. The less of a surprise it is, the easier it will be to handle if it actually happens to you.

The world is full of economic indicators. Press and television bombard us daily with details on how the country is performing. Tell-tale signs are all around us, wherever we work. It's not just the managers and executives who have access to this information – they just have more of it and, on some occasions, it is in a more convenient form. For them, comparing the monthly accounts with the corporate business plan should tell them exactly how the company is performing, but, whether you work on the shop floor, in the accounts office or out on the road, you should know a good part of that information a good deal earlier than the bosses. Rising stock, reduced production, less overtime and short-time working give clues that things are not going too well. Empty order books mean that matters are likely to get worse. Problems with the deliveries of raw materials often mean that suppliers are not being paid. Blitzes on overdue accounts are often a sign of pressure from the bank.

Most companies will experience difficulties from time to time without it being necessary to announce wholesale redundancies. However, if the bank and suppliers are both playing up or if production and sales are both down, it is sensible to be aware that no business can keep going in exactly the same way when it's under pressure on several different fronts. If the market turns down, it's unlikely to be strong enough to survive; if the market picks up, suppliers are less likely to want to do business with it.

If business prospects don't look too good, start tuning in to those vibrations that will give a clue to your own survival hopes. Hard as people try, it's almost impossible for them to completely disguise their intentions. Perversely, changes for the better often precede opposite actions – for instance, the boss who turns from animal to angel overnight is only trying to come to terms with their conscience.

Changes in routine are often the most significant indicators, but these can, sometimes, be quite subtle. Questions asked out of context, meetings arranged at unusual times or in uncommon places should all be accompanied by a 'Why'? Increases in social conversation, discussions about the detail of current projects, unrelated exchanges on the potential of subordinates – all should be treated with suspicion.

Company reports and accounts

Almost all limited companies are required to file annual accounts. Copies of these can be obtained, for a small sum, from Companies House, Cardiff, or through commercial search agents. The difficulty with company accounts is that they are historical documents, which have been prepared to satisfy a particular legal requirement and so, often, they require expensive expert interpretation. Recurring losses, however, are easy to understand.

One advantage of published accounts is that they can demonstrate the underlying strength of an organization and signpost future problems. Big cars and small salaries might be intended to create the illusion of substance; an expiring lease could herald an imminent move or an unacceptable increase in overheads; a freehold site might well exceed the value of the business as a going concern.

Company accounts can also give an insight into the way management might approach an issue as they are a record of the way they have previously acted, although what they've done in the past is, of course, no absolute guarantee of future behaviour. For example, if the directors have been buying cars for cash in 'bad' years or making substantial contributions to their pension funds rather than investing in much-needed new production plant, then the business may have limited long-term prospects.

Quoted companies (those whose shares are traded on the Stock Exchange) often compete to produce the glossiest and most striking document. Firms of accountants even offer awards for the quality of information that they contain. But, as most are actually groups of companies, there is rarely much information of value in the accounts themselves. For the interested researcher, however, the most useful source of information is generally the Chairman or Chief Executive's report.

Although the company report is necessarily upbeat (share dealers savage those that are not!), there are often clear signals as to how the different parts of an organization have performed. 'Again', for example, is generally the worst word to accompany substandard performance as it means that the CEO is admitting that something which went wrong two years ago has still not been put right. Of course, the statement will say something euphemistic, along the lines of 'the production division *again* encountered severe trading conditions as a result of the continuing recession . . .', but the message behind this 'again' for the managers (and, possibly, the whole workforce) could mean the same – the sack.

Rationalization and reorganization

Rationalization *should* be the consequence of the ongoing management of any dynamic organization, but has, unfortunately, become almost extinct in practice. Managers who should constantly be seeking ways of improving business efficiency display a marked unwillingness to address the issue on a routine basis, preferring to allow a crisis to develop first. The wave of job losses that followed the privatization of many previously nationalized industries emphasizes the difficulty of making predictions in this area. Overmanning was a fact of life, in the past, but managers were reluctant to precipitate confrontation with strong trade unions. The sea change in attitudes that followed the sales to investors resulted in hundreds of thousands of job losses.

Perhaps it is fair to conclude that few redundancies are likely to result from any continuous assessment of the way in which an organization conducts its business, provided that the company remains in the same ownership.

Reorganizations come in two forms:

- the real
- the spurious.

Plans that improve the efficiency of an organization's service delivery or lead to a reduction in its unit production costs are legitimate and valid, but frequently lead to job losses. They are, quite often, associated with a 'global review of the business', which should, in itself, be enough to set alarm bells ringing in certain sectors. Few commercial concerns are likely to commission a study that results in *no* cost savings, after all. The appointment of consultants, therefore, is the most obvious sign that something is afoot – though quite *what* is sometimes difficult to tell. It is, perhaps, cynical to suggest that any director who needs to appoint a firm of accountants to advise on the conduct of the business (the majority of business analysts are accountants of one form or another) is hardly worth their job title.

This brings us to the use of consultants in the *spurious* reorganization. This also takes two forms and both usually result in job losses. The first is simply a device that allows bosses to be disassociated from their intentions as the consultants will do what they're told and employers will distance themselves from the consultants' conclusions. This technique is particularly useful where an organization is to be reduced in size and responsible executives wish to maintain reasonable relations with remaining employees.

The second form of spurious reorganization is more specifically targeted. In this case, the roles of selected individuals are retitled and their existing posts are made redundant. It's quite lawful, though hardly moral, and often intended to precipitate the departure of the affected individuals before any redundancy payment becomes due.

Bids and takeovers

Agreed bids are often better for the directors than for the shareholders or workforce. After all, self-preservation is the strongest instinct.

An agreed bid generally acknowledges that the acquiring company can manage the business better than the incumbents. While this does not always mean bad news on the jobs front, there will frequently be areas of overlap in areas such as marketing and central administration. Often, it's simply a matter of waiting to hear what the acquiring company has to say, although, if the organization is quoted, there may be some indicators in the last annual report from the Chairman of the acquiring company.

Hostile bids aren't any easier to predict. The offer and defence documents are usually filled with so much rhetoric that one is left wondering how either company has actually managed to survive in business so far! Reading between the lines is essential in such cases. Whereas the bid will generally focus on past performance and the defence of future prospects, both are likely to include some measurable performance indicators.

If either organization makes claims, it should be possible to make comparisons between these and the information contained in the last published accounts. If, for example, the bidder claims that its cost of sales figure is 20 per cent lower than that of the target company, it might be because it's simply a bad payer, but, if it's not a bad payer, then redundancies could be in the offing, whether the bid is successful or not.

The usual defence is that 'we're already doing that', or, 'we'll be doing that soon'. So far as quoted companies are concerned, they'll be expected to do what they say or face the wrath of the City institutions.

APPENDIX: THE DANGER SIGNS

The pen is usually mightier than the sword

Most directors of public companies are sensitive to the views expressed about them and their companies in the media generally and, particularly, in the financial press. Adverse comment can depress the share value, which affects the attitude of the investing institutions and, ultimately, directors' incomes.

If a financial journalist or share analyst offers valid criticism, the company will be expected to react. So, if the comment refers to 'losses in the widget division', then everyone in that division can expect changes. These could range from the replacement of the Managing Director to closure of the entire operation. Often, the correspondent will helpfully offer their own solution.

Nothing is so certain as change

Changes in the highest echelons of management are, fortunately, quite rare, but when they do happen, they can have profound effects throughout an entire organization.

There are two distinct types of operator in this field. The first is often followed by the key players from the same executive team that helped forge the manager's reputation. This is instant bad news for the existing directors, but may be less so for the remainder of the employees. Usually, such high-profile appointments come with a complete analysis of both the problems and the solutions. If you're part of the problem, though, don't wait for a gold watch.

If an organization exists, it is because of its people. If it's in trouble, it's because of some or all of those same people. At best, most of them will be in a narrow band spread either side of average who can be trained and motivated to perform at an acceptable level. Only a few will fall short of what are adequate levels of performance.

The alternative style of manager will concentrate on motivation and performance, but will be no less ruthless when it comes to excizing incompetence. Rather than bringing their own team of 'star' performers, therefore, such a manager will concentrate on getting the best out of the existing people in the organization. This style will then be expected to percolate down through the other managers and executives and so could result in redundancies at every level.

APPENDIX: THE DANGER SIGNS
Discretion is the better part of valour

Interpreting any kind of information has risks, but interpreting pieces of the data in isolation compounds that risk. Remember that there are no prizes for upsetting the management – British industry has a long track record of shooting the messenger. Try to be aware of what's happening in the economy in general, your industry in particular and specifically in your company.

It is, perhaps, a sad reflection on our times that companies are more concerned with the PR aspects of mass redundancies than the human consequences for those who are most directly affected. Countless thousands of job losses have been announced as being achieved through 'voluntary redundancies, natural wastage and early retirement'. It actually seems easier to talk about cancer and AIDS than to admit that you're forcing people out of work.

Commentators never ask how many lives will be ruined as the result of redundancy, how many suicides there'll be, how many mental breakdowns, how many debilitating physical conditions will result, how many marriages will break up or how many children will become dispossessed and alienated as a result. How common is the dismissal of those directors who allowed the situation to develop? There is a conspiracy of silence. Redundancy has taken the place of illegitimacy and mental illness as the subject no one talks about.

There is a school of thought, one that embraces many politicians, that looks on the unemployed as mere cogs in a wheel. The idea, which still prevails three quarters of a century later, was first popularized by Henry Ford, who turned farm labourers into assembly line workers. The concept offers a 'formula' solution for unemployment, a 'quick fix'. The idea that you can retrain and find work is, sadly, no longer the whole answer. This is because unemployment does not only affect the 'labouring classes'. Nowadays, it's just as likely to be a lawyer or surveyor who has been made redundant as a miner or steelworker. As neither the State nor the most sensitive of employers have found ways in which to resolve this problem, you need to do it for yourself.

Although this book has laid bare the often devastating consequences of redundancy and unemployment on individuals, their partners and their families, we hope that it has also shown that it is possible to survive the experience of being thrown out of work, and even to grow and develop both personally and in a partnership.

Teamwork and the ability and willingness to change and adapt are the keys to survival and success.

Further reading

Books about redundancy and unemployment:

From the library:
Finn, Dan and Murray, Iain, *Unemployment and Training Rights Handbook*, 3rd edition, an unemployment Unit Guide, 1995.

From bookshops or the library:
Bramham, John and Cox, David, *Job Hunting Made Easy*, Kogan Page, 1995.
Cane, Sheila and Lowman, Peter, *Putting Redundancy Behind You*, Kogan Page, 1993.
Golzen, Godfrey, *Going Freelance*, Kogan Page, 1993.
Ingham, Christine, *Life Without Work*, Thorsons, 1994.
Woolf, Jenny, *Redundancy, Coping and Bouncing Back*, Piccadilly, 1995.

For interviews:

Nierenberg, Gerard I. and Calero, Henry H., *How to read a person like a book*, Thorsons, 1984.
Pease, Allan, *Body Language*, Sheldon Press, 1992.

Books about relationships:

The RELATE bookshop at Herbert Gray College, Little Church Street, Rugby CV21 3AP, publishes lists of books on several subjects, available by post. Write for details.

From this I recommend:
Litvinoff, Sarah, *The RELATE Guide to Better Relationships*, Vermilion, 1992.

Also:
Cozens, Jenny, *To Have and to Hold*, Pan, 1995.

Useful addresses

Association of Consulting Actuaries
1 Wardrobe Place
London EC4V 5AH
0171-263 5514

Association of Citizens Advice Bureaux
Myddelton House
115–123 Pentonville Road
London N1 9LZ
0171-833 2181

Abbeyfield Society
186–192 Darkes Lane
Potters Bar
Herts EN6 1AB
01707–44845

Asian Family Counselling
74 The Avenue
Ealing
London W13 8LB

Catholic Marriage Advisory Council
1 Blythe Mews
Blythe Road
London W14 0NW
0171–371 1341

Debt Counselling
National DebtLine – 0121–359 8501
Money Advice Centre
318 Summer Lane
Birmingham B19 3RL

Drinkline
National Alcohol Helpline 0345–32 02 02
London – *0171–332 0202*

USEFUL ADDRESSES

Jewish Marriage Council
23 Ravenshurst Avenue
Hendon
London NW4 4EL
0181–203 6311

Rapport
1A Forum Buildings
St James' Parade
Bath BA1 1UG
01225–448343

Ramblers Association
1–5 Wandsworth Road
London SW8 2LX
0171–582 6878/6826

RELATE
National Marriage Guidance
Herbert Gray College
Little Church Street
Rugby
CV21 3AP
01788–573241

SAMARITANS
One national number: *0345–90 90 90*

Westminster Pastoral Foundation
23 Kensington Square
London W8 5HN
0171–937 6956

Recruitment consultancies

Witcher-Stronge Selection
Tarrant House
Christchurch Road
Virginia Water
Surrey GU25 4BE
01344–845 550

USEFUL ADDRESSES

Drake Beam Morin Plc
5 Arlington Street
London SW1A 1RA
0171–493 8444

Sanders & Sidney Plc
Orion House
Upper Street
London WC2H 9EA
0171–413 0321

Index

actuary 14
Association of Consulting
    Actuaries 14
advisory services 68
affairs 21, 22
age 100
alcoholism 19
alcohol counselling 75
anger 26, 35

benefits 68
bereavement, comparison with 39
business start-up 54
B&Q 100

Citizens Advice Bureaux 68
change 27
children 24
compensation 13
competency profiling 70
computers 46
confidence, loss of 16
contractual entitlements 13
coping: capabilities 16; coping as
    a couple 16
counselling 71
curriculum vitaes, CVs 69

debt 65
depression 73
directories 47
doctor 74
Drinkline 75

economies 45
essential expenditure 46

exercise 75

family survey 83
fringe benefits 13

health 74
holidays 17
home working 55

impotence 20
improving changes 49

job applications, application
    forms 47
Jobclubs 70
job creation 54

libido, loss of 20
libraries 57
life without work 103
lists 45
limited company, setting up 54

mining communities 10
money 32
moving 83

networking 67

Orbach, Susie 63
outplacement counselling 69

patterns of behaviour 81
pensions 13
planning 58

questions, asking 41, 48

relationships: balance in 33; re-evaluation of 90; refresher courses 90
resentment 63
retirement, compulsory 38
roles 41
role swap 59

teamwork 43
telephone 30
threads analysis 70
trading down 52

understanding yourself 82

why should I? 63
working away 84, 91